MW00962000

FREED TO TELL

Breaking The Chains Of Abuse and Shame

By Sarah Bratcher

To Sharn
God bless you
in all
that you do !

love in
Christ .
Sarah
Bratcher

PRESS

Copyright © 2009 by Sarah Bratcher

FREED TO TELL
by Sarah Bratcher

Printed in the United States of America

ISBN 978-1-60791-366-5

All rights reserved solely by the author. The author guarantees all contents are original and do not infringe upon the legal rights of any other person or work. No part of this book may be reproduced in any form without the permission of the author. The views expressed in this book are not necessarily those of the publisher.

Bible quotations are taken from:

Scripture taken from the Holy BIBLE, NKJV (New King James Version) Reference Edition. Thomas Nelson Publishers Copyright © 1988 Thomas Nelson, Inc

The Holy Bible, New King James Version Copyright © 1982 by Thomas Nelson, Inc.

The New King James Bible, New Testament Copyright © 1979 by Thomas Nelson, Inc.

The New King James Bible, New Testament and Psalms Copyright © 1980 by Thomas Nelson, Inc.

www.xulonpress.com

DEDICATION

This book is dedicated to all abused and abandoned children
and those effected by any type of abuse.
Remember God loves you and there is Life After Abuse!

CONTENTS

ACKNOWLEDGMENTS

To those who make up the team of Life After Abuse I give my thanks for the love and commitment shown to this great ministry and greatly appreciate their endless supply of energy, patience, and endurance. My thanks go to Dove, Kathy, Lin, and also to Bernie, Lou, Phil, Ah, Denise and others who have graced our path through the years. I would like to give a special thanks to Dave, for the spiritual covering he provides for this ministry and for his prayers, guidance and support. I am also grateful for those friends God placed along my path and those who continue to give me wise and godly counsel.

I am so grateful to Kathy Penberthy, for giving selflessly many hours of her time to help me edit this book. I know that God brought her into my life and has used her in a mighty way in this endeavor. Through unending patience and expertise, the manuscript was brought to life and transformed into a readable work. I could not have completed this book without that assistance. I would like to thank Kathy for always allowing me to retain my own thoughts while gently guiding me through the grammatical structure. May God bless her in all that she does as she continues to serve our Lord and Savior, Jesus Christ.

I would like to give my sincere thanks, love, and appreciation for the support of my pastor, Wendell Rhodes and his wife Beverly for the positive influence they have had on me as well as their encouragement since I have been at Friendship Worship Center.

I want to thank my three lovely daughters, Shawn, Shannon, and Sherrie for never giving up on me even during those rough years.

I love them dearly and I am very proud of all three of them and want to share of the tremendous blessing they are in my life. God has also brought along seven lovely grandchildren, Ali, Kayla, Joshua, LizziAnna, Sarah, Richard, and Natasha, for which I am very grateful. I pray that He will become the center of all their lives as they learn to love Jesus themselves and in turn be a blessing to others.

I am grateful most of all to God for the privilege in being able to minister to His children in Life After Abuse Ministries International and for all those who are being set free by the power of Jesus Christ.

IN MEMORY

In memory and gratitude to my mom, Vivian Cooper who led me to the Lord and to my stepfather, BJ Cooper, whose positive spiritual influence gave me invaluable guidance through the years.

PREFACE

The first time I met Sarah was one morning late in April 2002. I was counseling at the church where I attended in Greenwood, South Carolina. She had been sent to me by the pastor of that church and I met with her in my office. She looked distressed; appearing as though she hadn't slept for days as she desperately related her story. By that time I had already been a counselor for some years and had worked with various clients and their problems. After talking with Sarah, who then wished to be called Faye, I discovered she suffered from MPD, commonly now known as DID, or Dissociative Identity Disorder. Dissociation is the mind's ability to splinter into several individual parts, often as a result of abuse or other trauma. Although I was familiar with this disorder, I had not previously dealt with anyone suffering from that particular problem.

We talked for at least four hours that day having a session in the morning and another late in the afternoon. The challenges that lay ahead were tremendous. Even with the complexity of what Faye faced, I knew with God's strength, wisdom, and truth that she could be set free from the bondages of her past. I began praying immediately that God would equip me in such a way that I could then minister to her. I felt that God, for some time, had been preparing me for such a challenge as this.

I began working with the personality, who called herself Faye, that afternoon in April. Approximately two weeks after first meeting her she prayed a prayer in my office surrendering her life, past and present, to Jesus Christ. She was then set free after almost a lifetime of being in bondage to her past which included abuse by others, self-abuse, depression and suicide attempts.

At that time Sarah (now known by her birth name) and another lady were running a secular internet site relating to MPD. As soon as she had made her commitment to Christ, I encouraged her to begin sharing in a more positive way about how she had gained her freedom. For a few months the site remained active and as Sarah related her experience there; she found the response was overwhelming. Those needing help were encouraged through the positive feedback on the message board. Some were referred to me and I corresponded with them by email.

In September 2002, after creating a room called 'Life After Abuse' on an internet chat network, Sarah was surprised by the first night attendance of thirty-five people. They came with names that depicted their struggles like 'No_hope_1', 'tattered memories' and 'hidden scars'. Thus this new ministry was born.

Six years later it continues to grow, with moderators from Canada, the USA, and the UK assisting her each Tuesday and Friday evening, as they provide support for others who struggle in areas of abuse. They provide focused studies that teach from God's Word and give hope for a better future.

Today, Sarah is one person, not the multiple personalities that her mind created. As you read her story, may you be encouraged by the power of Jesus Christ, the Great Bondage Breaker, who came to heal the broken hearted and to set the captives free.

David N Lindler
New Life Christian Counseling Center
Greenwood, South Carolina

The fear clutched at me then, gripping like giant invisible hands,
and driving me into the 'inner circle of safety'…

CHAPTER 1

Eternity Is a Long Time

My first recollection of loneliness was watching the lights of my mom's car as it slowly backed down the long graveled drive at my grandparent's house. I was young but don't remember exactly how young. I can visualize my closet full of expensive dolls that Mama bought for me. In my mind I can still smell the musty odor of the house where I stayed most weekends. If I listen carefully I can also hear the ticking of the Grandfather Clock, which sat on the beautifully carved mantle above the fireplace.

The stillness of the house, in those days, only exaggerated the beating of my heart. The fear clutched at me then, gripping like giant invisible hands, and driving me into the 'inner circle of safety' that I had created for myself. I can still see a little girl sitting on the carpeted floor in the middle of the guest bedroom that she had learned to call her own. That little girl was me. I sat quietly, surrounded by the only friends that were truly mine. I had a family of dolls there. I had built an imaginary fortress and place of safety and the only reminder of my ordeals, was the tall, four poster bed which stood as a hideous memorial to the things which took place there.

Sitting by all my dolls with their metal trunks filled with every type of wardrobe possible, I didn't have to think of anything else except how to enter their world. They were already a part of mine, but deep within me was the thought that maybe I could become a part of theirs as well. The question was how I could make sure that

I was able to keep them with me forever. I was young, but not too young to realize that at a certain age girls just didn't play with dolls anymore. I could already see that Susie, who was my favorite, was getting scratched. She had curly hair much like mine which made her even more special. I was constantly asking myself what would happen if Susie's arm fell off or even worse if the house caught on fire and all the dolls were destroyed. I secretly hoped if there was a fire that I would die also because I couldn't possibly imagine my life without my dolls.

One day, out of the blue, I devised a plan. It was so fantastic, so intriguing and complicated, that even I didn't understand its implications. All I knew was that it could work and, that if it did, I would be able to always keep my dolls with me, even after I was too old to play with them. After all, I had entrusted things to them that no one else knew about, and those secrets had to be protected at all cost. This magical plan had already been in operation for quite some time.

I can recall at a very early age being able to transport myself to places of safety whenever things weren't going well. I can see myself now floating near the ceiling in my bedroom. It seemed as if Papa was always present. He was the man that I had called daddy until my mom had remarried when I was four. My biggest challenge at that time was staying away from him. Since I was unable to do it physically, my safety was in my ability to escape into my imaginary worlds.

I see this curly haired little girl, with big brown eyes, as one who possessed something special even then. During the bad times I could, in my mind, float up to the ceiling. I felt so light, like a helium balloon bobbing up against the tiles. From there I could see the room just as it was. What made it so important was the fact that I was transported far away from the groping hands of the man with the hideous moustache. There I felt free, liberated, like a cloud that could form in any corner of the room, and could hover and hide. I felt the need to do this often.

My mind wandered back into the bedroom of the newly built house, which sat on seventy two acres of woods and farmland. I so hated the smell of the hall closet outside my bedroom, but it was important to me because it housed my dolls. They resided on each shelf in perfect order. Two trunks were lined up at the bottom half of the closet. One was solid red metal and the other was a peach color with several water stains on the top. I remember how much trouble I got into because of the water spots that had created them. I wasn't allowed to take food or anything to drink into the bedroom and on one occasion I had blatantly disobeyed. Thereafter, every time that I took the trunks out of the hall closet, I was reminded of what would happen if I did it again.

At the very top of my hall closet, sitting on the highest shelf, was a doll whose majesty outweighed that of all the others. Her dress was made of satin and she was the most expensive one that I owned. The rules were simple. I could look at 'Daffney' but could not play with her. This doll literally took my breath away and, because she was so delicate, I was not allowed to take her from the shelf when friends came over to play. The real truth was, that not many friends did visit and that suited me just fine. I could amuse myself for hours and, besides that, I so hated it when my friends would say those two dreaded words, "Let's pretend." That one statement in itself spoiled everything because it was very evident from the beginning that they didn't think the dolls were real, whereas I did.

The house was always so still at night except for the ticking of the Grandfather Clock. My bedroom was next to the bathroom, which made it very convenient. I could get out of bed, quietly tiptoe into the bathroom and later get back into bed without being detected. Nights were long, that is, what I could remember of them. It was then that I thought of scary and bizarre things, like being abducted by alien spacecraft and, the most frightening of all, my recurring thoughts about eternity. I would lie on my back looking at the shadows on the ceiling. They formed a mass of monster faces, realistic enough to scare any child. Deep within all those shadows came that taboo thought.

As a child I had a real problem with the word eternity. I just didn't understand it. The preacher at the big church where my mother and stepfather attended talked about it a lot. He told horrible tales of bad people burning forever and ever in hell, where the worm would not die and where there would be sounds of wailing and demons flying around, however, most of the time my fear was that I would be right there with them. I had been told many times by my grandfather how very bad I was. I kept thinking about the water-spot incident. Something else kept running through my mind during these times and that was the phrase about the 'Spotless Lamb of God'. I figured I hadn't much of a chance to make it to heaven, especially with those who possessed a track record so much better than I could ever hope to have.

No matter how many times the word eternity would cross my mind I could not figure out just how long that would be. My mind would not allow me to accept the forever concept and I began to think how impossible it would be to have no end. Everything had to have an end; the day, the carton of milk and Friday nights with my mom. How could something go on forever and ever? These thoughts would make my heart beat faster and my breathing would get more labored. Then I would feel this tingling in my arms and hands. The more I tried to stop thinking about eternity the more I would do it.

Suddenly I couldn't breathe. Dark thoughts began to crowd my mind and I had to sit up in bed. Beads of sweat would pour down my back, soaking into my flannel gown. Sometimes I would shiver uncontrollably. I felt alone as if I was in a forest, dark and forlorn, only hidden by the branches hanging from the towering trees. In order to cope, I tried to view the trees as armies of soldiers marching beside me proclaiming their victory cries.

Then without warning my thoughts returned to times in my bed. It was then that I found myself looking into the eyes of my grandfather as he stood beside me. The shadows made weird looking lines on his already wrinkled face making him look as if he had scars. This was far worse than the monster shadows that appeared on my wall. It was reality, not fantasy.

"Time to say your prayers," he would sternly say. "Yes, Papa, I would reluctantly reply." Then compliantly I would repeat, "Now I lay me down to sleep, I pray the Lord my soul to keep. If I should die before I wake, I pray the Lord my soul to take. Bless Mom and Dad, Mama, and Papa, Bonnie and Granny and everyone. Help me to be a good little girl. Watch over me through the night and help me not to be afraid. Amen." It was strange that when I became an adult I could still remember that prayer but, for a time, not what had transpired afterwards. It would be years later before I was able to recall clearly the incidences of my childhood.

Abuse happened as well as the nightmares and the dolls became my way of escape. When I was sitting on the floor at my grandparent's house it was like as if I was in this other world where I could wipe out everything that was going on around me. I began to have blank spots; times when I couldn't remember things. I was always getting hurt but couldn't remember how the accidents would happen. Mysterious cuts would appear on my arms and hands although I had no recollection of how they got there. My mom just said I was a clumsy child and she concluded I had developed that trait from my grandmother who, herself, was always falling. I made many visits to the doctor's office and I stayed sick constantly, mostly with stomach aches which caused me to miss school.

Our family doctor was one who made house calls but only in the city. Dr Poliakoff was an older man with a kind face but with a limp resulting from a stroke he had suffered some years before. I always sat nervously, anticipating the thump of his limp, realizing he would have finished with his previous patient and that it was my turn to go in. I was terrified of entering that examining room. His nurse was kind and friendly but I just didn't feel comfortable around men.

On one visit to his office I was asked to step out of the room. I knew that they were going to be talking about me and I carefully watched as the nurse went into another room. I cautiously crept towards the swinging door. I could hear the doctor saying that I was just going through a phase and would grow out of it. He seemed to be reassuring my mom. I remember thinking how much I wanted reassurance also, but didn't get any. When I realized they had finished talking and that the nurse would soon return, I scuttled away from the door of the examining room and hurriedly sat down. The doctor walked out with my mom by his side. She was dabbing her eyes with a tissue. I can remember thinking to myself, "Was I such a bad child that I even made Mother cry?"

My mom was a special lady and she married a special man. I was four when she remarried. It wasn't until I was twelve years old that I realized that the man I called daddy wasn't my real daddy at all. I do recall an event where I was sitting on his lap in a court room, with my arms around his neck and saying, "This is my daddy." I hadn't a clue at that age what it was all about nor why they told me a 'sandman' was coming and that I needed to go to sleep. I later found out that this was the occasion of their wedding at an aunt's house. I had become a bit obnoxious as any four year old might, and this was their way of persuading me to take a nap. There were a lot of people around and everyone was dressed up, but no one told me it was a wedding. I am not so sure that I would have understood that concept at that age anyway.

I have to say I was a bit confused early on. I had a new daddy but yet we, as a family, lived with my grandmother and her second husband, the man I called Papa. It was as if I had two daddies, one that I liked very much and one who was stern and snappy and always telling me that we had secrets that must be kept. There were a lot of secrets in our family and everyone whispered a lot. I found out that even whispers are loud enough for children to hear if they really want to. I didn't talk very much. I was the lost child so to speak; the one who needed to be seen but not heard, so most of the time I watched the adults around me and said nothing.

I was taken to church at a very young age. We attended the largest church in town. I felt so small and insignificant standing between the wide pews. The preacher was loud but I was accustomed to hearing loud talking, usually late at night when my grandfather would get angry.

My mom and dad slept in a small bedroom well away from mine and I wasn't allowed to go and disturb them when they were sleeping. I hated being in the big bedroom in the middle of the house because it was next to the room where my grandparents slept. Sometimes very late at night Papa would be saying really bad things to Mama and I heard him say more than once that he was going to kill her. At such times as this I just pulled the covers over my head and put my fingers in my ears. The night before we went to church would be when he was the loudest. I tried not to think of what was going on around me but instead focused on going to church. That was something I really enjoyed.

I was fascinated with the wide crimson curtain at the back of the church. Every Sunday I studied it, watching for any signs of God that might be there, because that is where I thought He resided. In my childlike mind I felt that if somehow I could get behind the curtain then maybe I could ask God to help me. I have to say that if a child were to have only two wishes, mine at that time would have been to go to school, to learn how to read and also to be able to get behind that curtain. I know now that childhood concepts of God often come through authority figures in our lives. My first concept came from a drunken man who abused me and my grandmother. I therefore had mixed emotions about God. I was hoping He would be more like the man my mom had married and less like my grandfather.

My daddy was funny and cuddly and whenever we went out he would buy me anything I wanted. On one shopping trip he bought me a tricycle just like the one I already had, simply because I asked for it. That gave me a bit of hope about the God behind the curtain. I loved chocolate ice cream and so he would buy me this whenever I wanted it, even if much of it would end up on my dress rather than in my mouth. When my grandmother took me out, however, she would get me vanilla ice cream instead and tell me it was chocolate that just happened to be white. I don't think I ever did grasp the truth of that one.

There was a big change in our living situation following my parent's announcement that they had found a house and we would be going to live in the country. My grandmother wasn't happy about this at all. She pointed her finger at Mother and told her that she was not going to take me away from her. On the other hand, I stood there wide eyed and thinking how great it would be to be out of the house and away from my grandfather. I didn't say anything, but my mind was shouting, "Yes, Yes, I want to go!" I know that my mom cried a lot that day. My grandmother was always making her cry and I hated it when that happened. I would go and pat her on the shoulder and tell her that I loved her. She would hug me tightly and tell me she loved me too.

I, as a child of course, had no idea what manipulation was or how it affected the people in the household. I knew that my grandmother had a way of getting what she wanted by making people feel bad or making them cry. She did that with everyone except for my grandfather. She would take me shopping and buy me beautiful dresses but

21

then she always warned me, "Don't tell Papa I bought this and we will put it in a special place for a while." Most of my newest dresses stayed in the trunk in my bedroom until it was considered safe to wear them. It didn't matter to me about the dresses. I hated wearing them because every time I wore one and went out with my daddy I would usually come back with chocolate ice cream on the front of it, which would send my grandmother into a rage. She could easily hit the same decibel level as my grandfather when she was angry, although she didn't use the same bad language.

My daddy would usually crack a joke or ignore my grandmother completely which only seemed to agitate her more. That was one of the things which made my daddy special. He laughed a lot and wasn't serious like the others in the house. How I longed to be able to laugh all the time but most nights there was nothing to make me happy. Instead my greatest desire became to escape pain and to transport myself to a place of safety.

Finally the day came when my mom, dad and I began packing. My nightmare was over. We were going to a new home; a place where I would be safe, a place where I wouldn't have to rise and hover, and a place where there would be no shouting or tears. In my mind, I smiled.

*The distance to our new house was short, and the first thing that I
noticed about that house was the size. It was tiny…*

CHAPTER 2

New Home

My excitement began to grow with each mile, as we drove to the location of the place where I would be living with my mom and dad. I can remember bouncing from one side of the back seat to the other as my anticipation grew. I noticed every landmark along the way and especially how far it was from my grandparent's house. My daddy was singing merrily in the front seat and my mom kept telling me to sit still as it wouldn't be long until we arrived.

We turned on to a winding road and pulled into a circular driveway. I thought, "Wow! This is a very big house." and then blurted out, "Mother, I didn't know it was going to be this big!" She explained to me that this wasn't our house, but that the lady who lived there would be our landlord. "A landlord," I questioned in my mind. I had never heard this term before and was wondering if this woman could possibly be like God, except that she would perhaps be wearing a dress. Maybe there was a god for everything. My mind began to wander back to my toy box at home and the prospect of even having a 'toy lord'. I also wondered if perhaps there was a 'dress lord' as well.

"We have to pay her, Claudette." my mom explained. "Now settle down, and please don't fidget so much." I didn't say anything else and knew that it was again time to be quiet. It was very evident even to me that my mind was racing at a very high rate of speed. This happened whenever I would get excited about anything.

On arrival we all got out of the car and walked to the front door of the beautiful rustic home. I noticed the flowers and the neatly kept yard and wondered if this lady would let me come and pick some of the blossoms for Mother one day. My dad knocked on the door and a rather heavyset lady with white hair answered. She looked down at me with kind eyes and smiled. "You have a beautiful little girl. " She invited us in and I looked around for any sign of children living there. There was none, but I was not at all unhappy about this because some of my previous experiences with children had not been too positive.

My mom told me to sit down quietly while the adults talked. I wondered if they would start whispering, but they were loud enough for me to hear every word, not that I was particularly interested. My daddy pulled out his billfold and gave the lady some money and then we got back into the car. I found out that the lady's name was Mrs. Fuller and Mother had instructed me to be sure to say "Yes ma'am", and "No ma'am", when I talked to her. As we were getting into the car, Mrs. Fuller said, "Claudette, please come to see me sometime." She smiled and winked at me. I was thinking how nice she was, and I began to visualize a beautiful bouquet of flowers for my mom from her garden.

The distance to our new house was short, and the first thing that I noticed about that house was the size. It was tiny. It was the smallest house I had ever seen. My daddy unlocked the front door and I got my first glimpse of our new home. As we walked in, I immediately wanted to know where my room was. Mother explained that this house only had one bedroom so I would be sleeping in there with them. I know that my mouth must have dropped open and I totally forgot about how small this house really was. I was actually not going to have to sleep in a room of my own anymore. What more could a very frightened child ask for?

My mom and dad began to unload a few things from the trunk of the car, so I decided that now was the time to explore this place I was soon to call home. Our house sat in a semi circle with two houses to the right of it and one on the left. I quickly walked around the back and noticed a small screened porch overlooking a pasture with cows in it. As far as I could see was open land, so unlike the view from my grandparent's house where we had been living. They lived in the city and their back yard was small with little space for me to play. My mind began to race wildly as I thought of all the adventures I could have at my new home. I noticed a wooded area behind the pasture and thought of the prospects of making a secret hideaway one day, that is, if I was allowed to venture out that far.

These thoughts were interrupted by the voice of a boy who looked to be a little younger than me, shouting, "Hey, you gonna live here?" I pretended I didn't hear him and quickly walked around to the front of the house where my parents were still carrying boxes from the car. I gave a shy glance back at the boy who had followed me to the front porch. "Hey dork, I'm talking to you", he retorted. Now he had my attention. I glanced back again with a quick, "Yes, we are going to live here."

By this time the boy had walked over to me followed by a yellow dog. "My name's Donald, what's yours?" He paused. "Oh, and this is Pup, my stupid dog." "Claudette", I said, not taking my eyes off the dog that followed the boy closely. The yellow dog was dirty with a matted coat and he approached me excitedly and licked my hand.

"Stupid dog," snapped Donald as he ran to the edge of the yard, picking up a stick, and hitting the dog. The dog yelped a few times and then with his tail tucked between his legs, crept to the side of his house and lay down. I wanted to tell Donald that he didn't have to hit the dog and I wasn't afraid of it anyway, but I just stared and kept silent. This was my usual way of handling confrontations with people. I just turned around and ran back into our house. By this time Mother was opening the cabinets in the small kitchen and I heard her telling my dad that they would have to get some cleaning materials to bring out on the next trip.

In my thinking I was far more concerned about how I could stay away from Donald. I couldn't get the picture of him beating his dog out of my mind. I wondered if Papa also hit Mama when he got angry. I had never seen him hit her but I had certainly heard slapping noises from their bedroom many times. "I am not even going to think about this now," I comforted myself. "I have a new house, a fairly new daddy, and I no longer have to sleep in a room alone."

The most important thing to me was the fact that we wouldn't have to live with Mama and Papa anymore

I was warned several times not to mention the new house to my grandmother, when we went back home that day, as she was already upset about us leaving. She had tried everything she could think of to talk my mom and dad out of moving. I had, through my intuition, figured out the real reason she didn't want them to leave was the fact that they would be taking me away. She fumed and fussed about this a lot. My daddy would always use humor to deal with her ranting at times like this. On this occasion he teased her by saying that if they moved in with us they would have to be the ones to sleep on the sofa. She murmured something under her breath and stormed out of the room. I was just counting the days until we would actually be in our new home.

It was approximately two weeks later that my mom and dad moved the last pieces of furniture and belongings, into that tiny three roomed house. Everything was tucked away, as neatly as it could be, considering the fact that space was so limited. My most prized possessions, however, which were my dolls, remained at my grandparent's house. I was told that I could still play with them, when I went to visit, but that they had to remain there. My mom and grandmother had a very heated discussion because she refused to let me take the dolls. "I paid good money for those, "Mama hissed, "And I am not going to let her take them out 'there'. She referred to our new home as 'there' many times whenever she became angry.

On the day that we finally left, she handed me my favorite teddy bear, Casey, the one that I once thought I would never see again. This teddy bear held painful memories for me. One night, for example, when I was hiding from my grandfather and would not come out from under my bed, he grabbed Casey from the top of my toy box. From my position under the bed, I could see my grandfather's shoes and also the stuffing as it landed on the floor. He had ripped Casey apart. I tried to stifle the tears that ran down my cheeks. I stayed under my bed for quite some time that night, until I knew it was safe to come out again.

The next morning I gave the bear and the stuffing to my grandmother and asked her if she could repair him for me. I wondered if she realized that my grandfather had done this, because she didn't bother to ask me why Casey was in that state, but if she did know, she would have been afraid to confront him anyway. Now that I had Casey back this would have to suffice until I could also figure out a way to retrieve my dolls.

Suddenly I sat up. Excitement began to well up inside of me. I felt God. I knew that He was there…

CHAPTER 3

God of the Pasture

On the first morning in our new house I woke up startled. Everything was different. The smell of bacon being cooked reached me and I could hear the sizzle of my favorite breakfast food. My stomach told me it was time to eat but I lay there for a few more minutes, enjoying the absence of a morning inspection. I had been accustomed to being woken up early and given exactly five minutes to attempt to make my bed. There was also the issue of the shoes which had to be perfectly aligned in my closet, equally spaced apart from each other. At night I would always check to make sure everything was in place before I went to bed. Sometimes I would later lie there, trying to think of anything that perhaps I had forgotten. My grandfather was very thorough in checking under the bed, making sure that there was no debris left from the day before. I hated those times because inevitably something had been forgotten and that would mean a penalty would surely follow. There was great relief in knowing that those days were now past. I was so glad that my mom would let me sleep late. It was summer anyway and there was no deadline of having to be ready for school. My grandfather had the attitude, however, that nice little girls worked every day, summer and winter and so always needed a disciplined start to the day.

I was so tired the night before that I had fallen asleep on the sofa, while listening to the radio. My mom and dad were still busy finishing their unpacking, so Casey and I had sat down to enjoy a program called 'Amos 'n Andy'. It was evident from my parent's constant chatter, that they were having difficulty finding a place for everything. According to my dad we were already packed together like sardines. I sat there thinking how much I enjoyed being an only child as I had no desire for a brother or sister. The idea of sharing my dad with someone else in the house, didn't appeal to me at all. In addition to that, there was no way I would have wanted another child to go through what I had, at my grandparent's house, and experience the same level of fear as me.

My thoughts at that moment were on how long I could get by with just lying in bed, rather than getting up and starting the day. I looked at my wardrobe which sat in the corner of our bedroom. This was something that was truly mine, not like the dolls that I had to leave behind. I missed Susie, Terry, Baby Linda and all the others. I kept trying to recall how they were dressed the last time I had played with them. Had I remembered to put on their sweaters? At times it was very cold there and on more than one occasion I had felt what seemed to be a cold wind traveling through the house. Those incidences always seemed a bit frightening to me. I mentioned this to my grandmother once, and she said it was ghosts passing by, who would come and eat rotten little kids if they didn't do what they were told.

I hated the stories of ghosts. Once when I was at my Aunt Grace's house, my uncle had picked up a broom, placed a sheet over it and carried it past the window, as I sat sulking in the tub with soap and a dry wash cloth. Later my cousin Barry, their son, told me that this had been done to him as well, but he had figured out what they were up to almost immediately. He was good at letting me in on their little secrets, which gave me an edge on the adults who were making up the stories.

Barry and I had a great relationship. He was more like a brother than a cousin to me. Mother and I had lived with him and his parents for a year after moving from Columbus, Georgia where I was born. When Mama and Papa moved to Abbeville, however, my grandmother persuaded us to move in with them. I missed being out in the country with Barry. He picked on me unmercifully at times, but we did do a lot of fun things together. The other attractions were that the rules were more lax at my aunt's house than they were with my grandparent's, plus there was the advantage that my grandfather didn't live there. At the time of leaving Barry, it had seemed as if all the things that I loved the most were being taken away from me.

"It just isn't fair," I thought, as my mind returned to the present. The dolls were my family and I had not been allowed to bring them with me. It wasn't as if my grandmother would be bothering them, but could I say the same about my grandfather? Chills went up the back of my neck as I again thought of the night that Papa had ripped the stuffing out of Casey. I reached over to hug my bear just a bit closer and was thankful that at least I had him back in one piece again.

I wasn't quite sure what to do with the freedom I now had at our new home. Maybe I would celebrate by bouncing on my bed at some point, although the thoughts of what happened when I tried that at my grandparent's house made me shiver. And it might not matter at all, if the covers on my bed weren't perfectly straight, or maybe no consequences would follow either if my shoes were not perfectly lined up in my wardrobe. I did so hope that life would be different here.

The one closet in our tiny house was set aside for my mom and dad's clothes, so mine were kept in a newly bought piece of furniture. There was a place to hang my dresses, and drawers much like those in my doll trunks. I wasn't likely to get water spots on this one, and even if I did, I knew that my parents wouldn't make a fuss like my grandmother had done. My mom rarely raised her voice and most of the time my dad was smiling and making people laugh with his funny stories.

How I loved it when the two words 'my daddy' came to mind. The fact that they seemed to belong together made me smile inside. These warm thoughts were interrupted by seeing my mom standing in the bedroom doorway smiling, "Breakfast is ready sleepy head," she announced. I jumped out of bed and, out of habit immediately began to straighten the covers. Mother informed me that as the food would be getting cold we could make the bed together after I ate. Without wasting any time, or giving my mom an opportunity to change her mind, I grabbed Casey and headed for the kitchen.

He was going to be my best buddy until I could get all the 'others' back. I loved Casey, but I hadn't entrusted as many secrets to him as I did to some of the others. I knew that no detail, for example, got past my three faced doll. It was strange about that nameless doll. We had a 'love-hate' relationship. My grandmother had given her to me at one of my birthday parties. She was different from any of my other dolls in that she had a knob on top of her head, which could be rotated. This allowed me to change her face from a laughing one, to a crying face or a sleeping face. She wore a bonnet which hid the other faces from view. Many times I would change her to the sleeping face and tell the other dolls that she had died. They would be lined up on the floor by my bed and would be wearing their darkest outfits. There was something about that doll that frightened me and yet I seemed to be drawn to her. I wasn't sure why she came to mind now, except for the fact that I couldn't remember what face I had left her with, when we moved.

My mom and I sat and talked while I ate crisp bacon, scrambled eggs and steaming grits with extra butter. The toast was a bit burnt but that didn't matter. This was a new day and there was a whole new world out there, with much to be explored. Life was getting better by the minute; because right after breakfast Mother told me that I would be allowed to go out into the pasture. I was not, however, to wander far from the house nor go near the cows. My mom also suggested that I needed to be careful where I was stepping in the pasture. I giggled at this thought and went to change into my play clothes.

There was a barbed wire fence that separated our small back yard from the wide pasture. My mom carefully pulled two lengths apart so that I wouldn't get scratched when I climbed through. She had also prepared a container of juice, some apple slices and a few animal crackers, which were my all time favorite snack. She handed Casey to me and the picnic bag, once I was safely through to the other side, and had even thought of a small pink and white flannel blanket for me to sit on. She also gave me an old 'McGuffey Reader' and hinted that this would be a good time to practice sounding out my words. I had become fairly proficient at reading by then, which demonstrated that one of my wishes had already come true, that of being able to go to school and learn to read. I still had not managed to get behind the wide curtain at church to find God, so I continued to try and make that wish come true also.

Mother's final warning was to not venture out too far, or forget the time, as it would make me late for lunch. She leaned over to give me a kiss. I watched her as she disappeared into the house. "This is great!" I thought. Free at last, I could explore to my heart's content. In the distance the cows were grazing at the far end of the pasture, so I felt safe. It had been a long time since I felt that way, and my realization of having a wide and open back yard was liberating.

My eyes were on the woods that were just visible at the far end of the pasture. I so wanted to get into that forest. I had been fascinated with trees since the first time I saw pictures of them. I could recall sitting in a chair at my grandfather's barber shop, long before I could read, and gazing in wonder at the trees illustrated in the magazines there. They all seemed to be so stately, calm and strong. So began my daydreaming that warm morning in July. I knew that venturing into the woods wasn't a good idea, but in my mind I would be able to go anywhere I wanted. After all, one of my favorite pastimes was to daydream and I was getting skilled at the art of escapism.

I walked as far as I thought would be permissible, spread out my little blanket, sat and put my snack and book down beside me and rested Casey on my lap. I looked up into the cloudless sky. Even though the woods themselves were out of bounds, I could in my mind go there, in a similar way as I had, when I would bob about near the ceiling at my grandparent's house. Only this time I wasn't running away from anyone. The thought of nights at my grandparent's house was making me feel cold even though it was a warm summer's day. In order to escape those unpleasant memories I returned to dwelling on the happy thoughts that came from being among all those magnificent trees.

There seemed to be an invisible force drawing me into those woods. In my imagination I followed the winding pathway leading to tall pines, which formed an archway as they leaned intimately towards each other in an array of greenery. This particular spot was special, almost mystical. It was as if this archway was opening the way to a new dimension for me. I could visualize myself melting into the scenery, becoming one with nature. The thought brought me infinite peace as an inexpressible calm filled my soul. For a moment I longed to inhabit this place forever.

I passed a splintered stump. Across from it was an old log, now caked with dirt. I picked up a stick and began frantically scraping, searching desperately for something, much like I had under my bed at my grandparent's house. My mind threatened to dwell in that 'time-warp' but I couldn't let it remain there. That would have been too painful. No way did I want to return to that place.

As I mentally progressed deeper and deeper into the woods, I made sure that my thoughts went no further than my safety zone. The more that I practiced this technique, the more accomplished I became. I feared that a visit to my grandparent's house may have been imminent and, even with my mom there with me, I might need to use that acquired skill in order to block out the 'secrets' which I could never tell.

I continued my walk in the forest, but from experience had realized that going too far would have its' consequences. There were dark shadows lurking at a certain point and I didn't have the nerve to find out what lay beyond my hiding place. I always stopped short at this stage and so in my mind began climbing the hill that would lead me back out of the woods. I passed an old tire lying at the side of the pathway. It was filled with water and leaves. I tapped it gently with my foot as I walked by, careful not to disturb the soggy debris inside. The wind and rain had taken its toll. I began to wish that this same wind and rain could erase my memories as well.

In my journey I reached the archway, and without fear I walked beneath the towering trees. At that precise moment the giant limbs reached down and magically picked me up, lifting me high above the forest. As I looked down I found the scene had changed. The splintered stump, dirty log and old tire had all disappeared. Instead, I gazed upon a green forest, brilliant in color, the dew-laden leaves sparkling in the morning sun. The pine archway that had transported me was now missing also. Instead all the trees stood erect, their branches reaching upward, sending breezes of joy and serenity deep into my soul.

Suddenly I sat up. Excitement began to well up inside of me. I felt God. I knew that He was there. I looked up at the sky, across at the woods, the cows, the grass, and even Mother as she hung out the clothes in the distance. I knew from this moment that God didn't just stay behind that curtain at church. He was everywhere. And if He was everywhere, then that meant I didn't have to wait until Sunday in church to find Him. This was a great revelation to me. I had already become so aware of His presence on Sundays that there were times where I felt He might be writing down all the bad things that I had done, like not keeping my shoes straight or getting water spots on my doll trunks. It also occurred to me that God might be peeping out from behind that curtain to note the names of all those who didn't close their eyes during the prayers.

"What about prayer?" I thoughtfully questioned. I began to thank Him for the birds, the flowers in Mrs. Fuller's garden, my new home and my wardrobe, with at least two dresses that my grandmother sent with me. My list seemed to be endless and the more I prayed the more excited I became. I got up from my blanket and began running, flinging my hands about and laughing. It seemed that all I could say was, "Thank you". This was different from the other times when I had prayed my routine evening prayer. I still didn't understand that much about God, but felt I now had a fair idea as I ran around the pasture, that July day, He definitely knew about me.

My enthusiasm began to build and my thankfulness was so sincere, because it was coming from the heart of an innocent child. It would be many years before I would get the full concept of what God had done for me, but that day I was worshipping the Creator in my own childlike way. I sensed that God now smiled and He was riding on the wings of the summer breeze. At that moment I had experienced something which, some fifty years later, I would still be able to recall. I felt that in some way I had reached out and touched God, and I knew that He had touched me too.

I had become really proficient at taking myself outside of my body,
to escape the pain of dealing with the abuse from my grandfather…

CHAPTER 4

Unwelcome Visits

My morning revelation of realizing that God was in the pasture behind my house was interrupted by the bark of a dog. I had already seen Donald, the boy from next door; pick his way between the strands of barbed wire in the fence. He was now running towards me with Pup at his heels. I quickly leaned down to my blanket and picked Casey up, just in case the dog might possibly grab him for a plaything. Chasing a dog with a stuffed bear in his mouth was definitely not my idea of a fun pastime.

Whose black Buick is that in your driveway?" Donald blurted out. I just stared down at the blanket and cleared my throat. "That's Papa's and Mama's," I mumbled, a bit awkwardly. My thoughts were racing wildly now as two things crossed my mind. I wondered first of all why they had chosen this particular day to visit but, as I looked down at my Mickey Mouse watch, I thought perhaps Papa had taken an early lunch break and that hopefully they wouldn't be staying long. My second thought was that, even more importantly, my grandmother might now have had a change of heart and decided to bring my dolls to me. The thought of seeing my dolls again made me want to shout for joy, but instead I just told Donald I had better get back to the house.

Before I could pick up the paper bag containing my morning snack, Donald had reached over and snatched the animal cookies out of it and began feeding one to Pup. "Thanks for the grub, Claudie."

He threw the plastic bag of apple slices up into the air and caught them with his teeth and shook them around like a dog would do with a piece of meat. I thought that maybe he and Pup had been together so long, Donald was beginning to act like his dog.

I just stood there looking on with shock and amazement that he could be so rude. Although I wanted to tell him what a rotten kid he was, all I could do was to pick up my bottle of juice and my blanket, which I threw over my shoulder, and began walking slowly back to my house. This was not turning out to be a very good day after all, well not unless I found the dolls in my bedroom.

Just as I reached the fence Papa came around the side of the house. "Hey there Claudette, how's Papa's little girl?" "Not so great now," I thought, as I threw my blanket and juice container over the fence. I was still holding on tightly to Casey as I stared at the thin man with balding hair and mustache. Papa always wore the same attire which was dark pants and a white dress shirt. I shuddered inside, as he approached to separate the barbed wire so that I could crawl through. Mama had trailed behind him and held out her arms for a hug. She came over and drew me tightly to her. I could see Donald out of the corner of my eye snickering. He was feeding Pup the rest of my animal cookies while he snacked on a few as well.

My encounter with God seemed such a long time ago as I was ushered into the house by my grandparents. "Mama", I asked impatiently once inside. "Did you bring my dolls?" "No, I did not!" she emphatically replied. "They are right there at our house, waiting for when you come to spend the weekend with us. You can play with them on Saturday."

I am sure that most of the color drained out of my cheeks. I stood there rather dumbfounded for what seemed like an eternity and for a child who didn't embrace the word eternity, it certainly sure appeared to be a long time. At that precise moment my mom came from the kitchen still wearing her oven mitt and announced that lunch was ready. We all took our places at the yellow, oblong table. I sat quietly, picking at my portion of the casserole which my mom had prepared. The thought of food and spending the night with Mama and Papa was not a good combination.

The main topic of conversation was the fact that my grandfather had now purchased a seventy-two acre plot of land, and he would be building a house there. Papa didn't say much. In a group like this he was a bit more reserved. It became clear that the reason he was off work, at this time, was to finalize his loan from the bank. There were a lot of details I didn't understand but one thing I was sure of was my resolve to avoid going there for the weekend. Now, however, wasn't the time to plead my case with Mother. I had learned from experience how she always lost arguments with Mama and this time was probably not going to be an exception.

Mama talked incessantly while my grandfather, Mother and I listened. With Mama it was difficult to get a word in edgewise although when Papa drank it was then she who was silent. I was not in the least interested in hearing about buying land and house building. All I could think about was the fact that Mama had said I was going to have to spend the weekend with them. I was almost sure that my mom and dad wouldn't be going with me and so I would be alone with Mama and 'him'.

During the meal I excused myself and slipped into the bathroom. I felt sick and my heart was beating wildly. Somehow I had to get across to my mom and dad that I could not go to my grandparents'. I just needed to wait for the perfect timing. I stayed in the bathroom as long as I could, without having to be called back to the table. When I finally returned, Mama and Papa were getting ready to leave. My grandmother was telling my mom that she would pick me up at about noon on Saturday and to be sure to pack my clothes for church. I kept fighting the urge to scream out, "I won't be coming, so you don't have to make the trip out here!" All I could do was to stand there shyly and give each of them a kiss on the cheek before they walked out of the door. My kisses to my grandmother and grandfather were 'duty' kisses and not the generous ones that I gave my mom and dad.

Mama and Papa were gone now and, as much as I wanted to say something to my mom about the weekend plans, it was as if the words were stuck deep within my throat and I couldn't get them out. No amount of will power would drag those words out of my mouth. I stared down at the floor as if it was going to be possible to somehow conjure up a magician who could aid me in getting the word 'No!' out. "You are awfully quiet," Mother observed as she busied herself clearing the table and preparing to wash the dishes. "Want to help me dry them?" she asked. "Yes ma'am," I politely responded.

For the rest of the day, I sat on the front porch and watched Donald play with his dog. He came over a few times to try to annoy me but I just sat with my McGuffey Reader, pretending to be absorbed in my book. My mind wasn't on sounding out my words; however, but rather on how I could escape the weekend terror to come.

The only high point of that day, other than my encounter with God, was my dad coming home from work. He picked me up when he came through the doorway and swirled me around a few times. "Wow, not going to be able to do this much longer", he laughed. "Is your mother feeding you bricks?" He always had a way of making me laugh, no matter how bad the day had been. I was glad he was there.

That night I had a horrible nightmare. In it I was being chased through this huge house, with lots of rooms, by my grandfather. In most rooms there were no windows, but the few that did have windows had bars on them. I awoke in a panic, crept out of my bed and went to mom and asked if I could sleep with her and dad. She told me that everything was fine and to please go back to my own bed. She also reminded me, that I was already in the same room with them and so had no reason to be afraid. My dad later told me that, from then on, I approached his side of the bed whenever I was afraid, because he would give in to my wishes and let me sleep there. On this night, however, I lay awake for what seemed like hours trying to fall back to sleep, because I feared I may end up in the same nightmare as before. I was painfully aware that an even bigger nightmare was on its' way this weekend, and I didn't know how to stop it.

It wasn't until Saturday morning that I finally got the courage to say something. My mom had retrieved a small suitcase from my wardrobe and was looking through the drawers, when I finally spoke. "Mother I don't want to go!" I said in a pleading tone. "Please don't make me go!" My mom looked startled. "Claudette, I thought you loved Mama and Papa. It would hurt their feelings if you didn't visit them, "she replied as she continued packing. I could no longer suppress my emotions. I began to cry. She stopped what she was doing and sat down on the edge of my bed. "Look, you will only be there for one night and will be back here again on Sunday afternoon and in the meantime you will get to play with all your dolls." "I am so sorry Mama wouldn't let you bring the dolls here but you know how she is." I wanted to scream, but all I actually did was to wipe the tears from my eyes. I knew that I had lost this battle and that any further display of emotion would be futile.

Thus began my plight, of regular weekend visits to my grandparent's house. My only solace was the fact that I had five days with my mom and dad in between these visits. They were days of feeling safe and I especially enjoyed Friday nights when I shared the sofa with my mom, a blanket between us, listening to programs on the radio like 'Amos 'n Andy', 'I Led Three Lives', and 'Fibber McGee & Molly'. My weekends, on the other hand, were spent daydreaming and going to far and distant places. I had created places of safety in my mind, where I was transported deep into forests and even to faraway lands. There I could become a princess, being waited on by servants and wearing royal gowns like Miss Daffney Dupont wore.

I became withdrawn and sullen and rarely smiled on weekends. It was then that my elaborate plan of floating to a place of safety would come into play, as I had become really proficient at taking myself outside of my body, to escape the pain of dealing with the abuse from my grandfather.

*My only means of survival was to escape in my mind
and for part of me to hide beneath the neatly folded towels
in the cabinet behind me, while yet another part hid in the
barber's pole outside his shop...*

CHAPTER 5

Crystallizing Events

Everyone has a crystallizing moment, which can either take them on a life journey of hope and peace or one of death and destruction. Mine came at the age of nine. Words and actions up to this point were insignificant, compared with what took place one late evening at my grandfather's barber shop. I had always been obedient to him and kept our secrets. But this wasn't a game anymore and it wasn't our 'time together' and I was no longer Papa's little girl. I became a woman that night in every sense of the word, not by personal choice but by force. I can remember my arms being pinned to the barber's chair and having a towel stuffed in my mouth. My only means of survival was to escape in my mind and for part of me to hide beneath the neatly folded towels in the cabinet behind me, while yet another part hid in the barber's pole outside his shop.

I had stayed with them on a school night which was unusual and don't even remember the reason why I wasn't at home with mom and dad. At the time of the abuse the pain was excruciating and I prayed that I would die. Even though God had shown up in the pasture behind my house, that warm July day, I felt He must be taking care of more important matters than mine during those few agonizing moments.

The next thing I remember was sitting at my desk, in school the next morning. I walked to the teacher's desk and told her I didn't feel well. She called my mom who picked me up from school. About thirty minutes later I was again in the doctor's office waiting nervously. My physical pain was intense but my emotional pain was beyond description. By then I had no recollection of what had happened the night before. I would later find out that blocking out painful memories is a defense mechanism, and was one that I had been doing for years. My mind would not allow me to recall the events of that night until many years later.

For me everything had now changed. I wasn't sure who I was anymore. My fear increased with every tick of the clock on the wall in the waiting room. What was I doing here and why was I hurting so badly? These were questions that would not have an answer for many years. At this particular time my agony was without rhyme or reason.

The doctor's examination didn't take very long. I don't know what he said to my mom, although they talked together for some time after I had been sent back out into the waiting room. When we left the doctor's office Mother drove to my Aunt Grace's house. On the way she kept silent and so did I. She finally spoke out, reassuring me that everything would be fine. On arriving at my aunt's I was told to go and lie down on the bed in Barry's room. I could hear them talking and, even though they were trying to speak softly, I heard my aunt say, "She is too young to be starting her period." I didn't know what a period was and at that time it didn't matter to me. I felt sick and just wanted to sleep, hoping that maybe on waking I would feel better. Christmas came and went but my fears didn't. They began to increase day by day. I went through the motions of everyday life but I felt hollow inside, and had no clue as to why I was feeling that way. The weekend visits continued at my grandparent's house and so did the abuse.

One Saturday afternoon Mama and I pulled up into the driveway of their newly built house. My grandfather walked out of the house to tell me that he had a surprise for me. We walked down to the barn and he told me to close my eyes. He opened the door, and when I opened my eyes again there before me stood a horse. This was to be my horse. I stood there wide eyed. To me she was beautiful but probably to the average person would appear a bit on the scrawny side. She was a little sunken in and it did occur to me that she could be ridden without a saddle. The most important thing was that she was mine. I didn't realize at the time that I was being enticed to keep coming for the weekend visits. Until then, I had been putting up quite a bit of opposition about going to my grandparent's house. Mother and Mama were constantly arguing about me not wanting to visit. Mama always won and each Saturday, with suitcase in hand, I was taken by my mom or picked up by my grandmother.

Maude, my horse, did make a difference. For about a year I lived for weekends when I could spend time with her, feeding her apples and riding around the yard. I had to some degree accepted my life, such as it was, including the abuse. There was always a place of safety in my mind where I could retreat and had become adept at doing this. I still played with my dolls a lot and rode Maude at every possible opportunity.

One Saturday afternoon I excitedly jumped out of the car and ran to the barn only to find it empty. My grandfather followed close behind me. He stood at the door of the barn, walked over to a shelf, reached behind it and pulled out a bottle. This is where he kept what he called his medicine. He also pulled out a long knife, carefully placed his bottle on a table, and stared at me. "Too bad about Maude," he muttered, not blinking an eye. "She kicked me today." "No horse is going to do that to me." "I know you loved that horse, but bad things happen when horses kick and also when little girls tell secrets," he added. Papa kept sliding his fingers along the blade of the knife. "Don't mention one word of this to Mama." She wouldn't believe you anyway." "And don't you dare cry because bad things happen to little girls who cry.

He walked out leaving me stunned, staring at the empty barn. I didn't cry except on the inside. Anytime I thought of shedding tears, the image of Papa standing by that table holding his knife and making his veiled threat came to mind. I finally left the barn, went into the house, making my way straight to the hall closet and retrieved my dolls. I again entrusted them with a secret I knew they would never tell.

On February 4th, 1956 a big event happened in my life. I was to be no longer the only child. My mom and dad became the proud parents of a baby girl, Bonnie Jean. This was a new experience for me. For almost 10 years I had my mom and dad all to myself, now things were changing and I wasn't sure how I felt about it. My grandmother warned me many months before my sister arrived, that I needed to understand that, after the baby was born, I couldn't expect my mom and dad to love me as much as they would the new baby. This was because I wasn't a biological child to both of them. I had no clue what that meant and was too shy to ask. I had learned many times that asking questions of adults often received answers that made me feel insecure, so I just shared this one with my dolls. I thought about looking this word up in the dictionary, but every time I had the urge to do so, I couldn't bring myself to follow through with it.

I would usually be content sitting on the floor at home, coloring or reading a book, but would always notice when my dad picked my baby sister up. Both my mom and dad spent far more time with her than they did me. I felt very left out. On weekends, my grandmother would always make sneaky comments of how much she and Papa loved me and that I was lucky to have them. "Your sister and your mom and dad are a family." "We are all you have," she would say manipulatively. "You had better love us, because when we are dead and gone you are going to be alone." "No one will ever love you like we do"

I was the one who at times wanted to be dead. I loved playing with my three-faced doll and could visualize myself lying in a casket when I selected her sleeping face. She seemed so peaceful. I wondered a lot about death and how it would feel. The only part that bothered me was about the place they called hell. If it truly was a real place, then I knew that I was going to go there, because of how bad Papa made me out to be.

Even in the midst of all the turmoil that I was experiencing, I never forgot my afternoon in the pasture praying to God. If He was anything like I thought He might be, then perhaps He would take notice of my situation and get my mom and dad to pay more attention to me. I always hoped that maybe I would one day feel Him again like I had on that summers' day.

We continued attending the big church in town and they had a lot of programs for young people. I joined Girl's Auxiliary and the pastor's wife, Mrs. Benjamin, was in charge of this group. Her daughter Susan and I were best friends. I had begun to enjoy the interaction with others of my age, much more so than I did when I was younger. We did a lot of fun things and projects. I joined Junior Choir and also went to Training Union on Sunday nights. I loved to sing and my mom also enrolled me for piano lessons with a teacher who lived near us.

My parents had long since moved from the tiny house they rented from Mrs. Fuller. I loved music. Mother played the violin and how I loved to listen to her play on Friday nights. She was an accomplished violinist. She would, on occasion, also read me a story she had written about Abram Dabosky, a pianist who went on tour. She related how at the end of each performance he would stand as the audience applauded him. In his mind's eye he could only see the face of his father who had died a few years earlier, saying, "Well done my son, well done." As many times as I heard that story it always came to me fresh and new. She told me if I practiced enough, that I could succeed in a similar way, but all I could think about was the part where the father died, which made me feel very sad.

I remember one particular Friday night when my mom was sitting on the sofa, Bonnie was asleep and my dad was taking a bath. She asked me to come and sit on her lap. I hadn't done that since my sister was born. She sang to me the song 'It Is No Secret'. I had heard her sing this many times but never while sitting on her lap. I lay my head on her shoulder as she began to sing. I drifted off to sleep, thinking how great it would be to always feel that secure.

In view of my experiences, I had mentally made a list of every woman leader in the church, who I thought I might be able to confide in. In reality, I could never get the courage to tell them how badly I felt so much of the time. The weekends at my grandparent's house had taken their toll on me, both physically and emotionally. I stayed sick with headaches or stomach aches, and since I had missed so much school I was only earning 'Cs' on my report card. One day after being severely reprimanded by my grandmother concerning my grades, I retreated into my bedroom at their country home. My dolls were lined up on the floor. I walked over to the dresser and there in full sight was a razor blade. I picked it up and pressed it into my hand, hard enough to bring blood. It hurt but at that moment I also felt a release. Thus began my days of self abuse which would last for nearly fifty years. I discovered unique ways of cutting without being detected, and found it just as freeing as hovering above my bed.

The victim didn't move. I can't now even recall if he ever cried out, but I did know he was dead.

CHAPTER 6

Terror in The Woods

There was no question about it, I was a troubled child. Mother's attempts to get me motivated were often to no avail. I would at times be happy and carefree but she often commented that at others I was very quiet and detached. We were in the kitchen one night immediately after we had finished drying the dishes. This was always my special time with mom, when she would ask me how my day went, and I actually looked forward to this time in the evening. This saved me being around my dad and watching him making a fuss of my little sister who had just started to walk. Every one walks at some time or another so I didn't see what the big deal was. I interpreted everything that my dad did with my little sister, as pushing me further and further out of his life. The words of my grandmother rang through my ears intrusively at such times as these.

That night there was a troubled look on Mother's face, and she began to ask me questions about my weekends with Mama and Papa. She observed that I always acted differently when I got back home. I so wanted to tell her how much I hated going there, but I was unable to voice my protest then, just as I couldn't when I was asked for the first weekend visit. I could not erase the picture of my grandfather holding that knife. It seemed that the warning I had received, concerning the fate of little girls who told secrets, would forever be etched in my memory. I placated Mother by telling her that everything was fine but I just missed being home with them at weekends.

She told me that Mama did a lot for me because she loved me so very much and the least that I could do would be to spend time with them. Mom explained that as Mama only had one child that she considered me as one of her own. I didn't like the idea of having two moms. It wasn't that I didn't love Mama and all the beautiful clothes that she bought me, but being with them wasn't worth all the concealing I had to do in my mind. I felt so different from my other friends. I wondered if any of them had secrets that they had to keep, and if so how they managed to hide them. Even though I wondered about this, I knew that I would never have the courage to ask them.

After I had gone to bed that night I thought a lot about what my mom had asked me and I felt disappointed that any opportunity for disclosure had been lost. She had given me the chance to tell her how horrible Papa was to Mama, and what he was doing to me, but I had remained silent. I remembered him telling me not to tell Mama because she wouldn't believe me anyway, and I was afraid my mom wouldn't either, even if I did gather the courage to tell her.

Two years later I had a rude awakening, making me aware that there was a dark side of life, much darker than any I had previously known. I was scheduled for one of my weekend visits, but this time Mama didn't come to pick me up as usual, but instead I was met by my grandfather. He didn't tell me until we were about half way back to the house that Mama would be working until midnight. She was a drawing-in hand at the mill in town and they were behind schedule, so she would not be coming home until midnight. My heart started beating very fast and, had the car not been going at a considerable speed, my first impulse would have been to jump out. I didn't say a word; however, because I realized that asking him to take me back home would have made no difference. I sat silent in the car for the rest of the way home.

Papa informed me that Mama had already prepared dinner and after we had eaten he would be taking me out somewhere. I began to panic. Even though I had managed to block the memory of the barber shop incident out of my mind, as well as the many other abuses, I knew that this latest plan of his couldn't be good. Never once did

I expect what would actually take place that Saturday night, when I was eleven years old. If I had been able to imagine any possible catastrophe it wouldn't have come close to what I experienced. Nothing could have prepared me for what would follow.

He said very little during dinner. We sat at the kitchen table which was only large enough for two. I spent most of the time staring down at my plate. "You not hungry tonight?" he inquired. "No Sir", I answered, not even looking up. He had finished eating and took my plate away without even asking if I planned to eat any more. He placed the dishes in the sink and told me to go and put on some play clothes, as we would be going out. I immediately obeyed. It was never wise to question Papa.

I was told we were going on an adventure and that it again would be a secret which could never be revealed. Those words didn't surprise me at all because I was use to hearing them. By this time secrets had become a way of life. At about 7:30 pm, just before dark, I walked out of the door with my grandfather. He carried a lantern and told me to follow him. We walked past the barn and on into the woods. With each step I took, my heart began to beat faster. The hike was long, through brush, trees and a barbed wire fence that had fallen over. As we approached a clearing, I saw a lot of lanterns and as we walked into the open I noticed a group of men standing in white robes with hoods over their faces. My grandfather told me to stay where I was and he walked over to one of the men. I couldn't hear what he was saying. My thoughts were to run away, but I didn't even know the direction of the house and so stood there as if I was a statue, afraid to move, afraid to run and even afraid to breathe.

I knew this group was the Klu Klux Klan. I had heard my uncles talk about them and their hatred of black people. Both of my uncles were members of the KKK and I wondered if they were among this group tonight. The Klan was here on my grandfather's land and I realized immediately that this wasn't somewhere where I wanted to be. I wondered why my grandfather wasn't also wearing a white robe because I knew how much that he hated black people. I, myself, just didn't understand why anyone could hate another person because the color of their skin was different.

Two of the little girls that I played with were black and daughters of a lady who we called Aunt Mary. She would iron for us and 'Cootie' and 'Booger Ball' would come with her. They were so sweet. I always snickered because of their nick names but they loved them and I had never called them anything else. We had lots of fun together playing with the dolls, when they came over. I liked them and it wasn't just because they didn't say, "Let's pretend." My thoughts were interrupted when Papa approached and motioned for me to go and sit on a nearby log. He said, "Claudette, I want you to watch carefully, because this is what will happen to you if you ever tell one of our secrets."

It was not a particularly cold night but I felt a chill go through my body, like an electrical shock, as I sat on that log. My wish was that I could still be sitting on mom's lap with her singing to me, but in reality I was in this dark, forbidding place. I tried to think of 'hovering' as a means of escape, but fear gripped me in a way that it had never done before. My mind began racing, trying to reach a place of safety. In order to do this I became a giant named Max, who I was able to visualize stomping through the woods, plucking up all the men in white robes and taking them away. I felt frozen in time and, at that moment, I even felt betrayed by the forest that was supposed to be my place of refuge.

After what seemed like hours, but was in fact only minutes, a man wearing a different style hood walked into the circle formed by the other men. He pulled behind him a black man with a rope around his waist. The black man looked terrified, much the same as I was at the time. Two men left the circle, walked over to the man, threw him to the ground and stood there kicking him repeatedly. I jumped up off the log and screamed out, "No!" as loudly as I could. That action was a mistake, because my grandfather grabbed me by the shoulders and abruptly pushed me back down onto the log. He told me that if I spoke one more word I would regret the day I was ever born. I was shaking all over and my heart felt as if it would burst out of my chest.

The men mumbled a few words and then another took out a knife with which he stabbed the helpless man about five times in the chest. I can remember putting my hands over my mouth so that

I would not scream again. The victim didn't move. I can't now even recall if he ever cried out, but I did know he was dead. Each of the men took turns in going over to the dead man and kicking him. With each kick my heart felt as if it would stop. I wanted to scream out, "He is already dead, and why do you have to keep kicking him?" I couldn't speak, however, or think, and at that time I truly wanted to die myself. This event was something I could never have expected and was difficult for me to comprehend.

I felt intense anger at my grandfather to the point where I wanted to make him suffer in some way. I knew at that moment in time, that he was just as capable of violence as those other men and feared that I would not have a chance. I was terrified of him and this was not the first time I just wanted revenge. Many times I had thought of the loaded gun he kept in a drawer beside his bed. I would fantasize about getting that gun while he was asleep and shooting him, but the fear of him catching me in the act prevented me from doing so. I was also afraid of going to jail if I carried out my fantasy and was then found out.

This event that autumn evening, was the most horrible thing I could ever have imagined, and I witnessed every detail. I wouldn't have revealed our secrets anyway, even if my grandfather had not taken me there that night. But now, with this horrendous image etched on my mind, I would have to find a way to wipe out the memory of that night forever. All I could do at the time was to shake uncontrollably and try to hold back the tears. I sat there for a few minutes while most of the men walked back up the hill. Two remained with my grandfather. One man got a blanket and began wrapping the dead man in it. My grandfather grabbed my hand tightly and we walked away from the scene. He looked down at me and said in a low voice, "Claudette, what you saw tonight you can never tell, but I want you to think about it for awhile."

He then took me to a clump of trees and near them was a mound of dirt, some shovels and a very deep hole. There was a ladder inside one end of the hole and he told me to climb down. "Papa, please, please, you can't bury me!" I pleaded. "I won't tell, I promise I won't tell!" He informed me that if I didn't do what he instructed he would force me to go down there anyway. He assured me that I wouldn't be buried but that he just wanted me to think for a while. His main concern was that I would never reveal the events of that night. My mind went blank and I obeyed.

When I got to the bottom of the hole I looked up pleadingly with tears running down my face. He cursed at me and told me he would return in an hour. I stood there horrified as he lifted up the ladder, leaving me trapped at the bottom of the hole. Then almost immediately I heard the clump of something being dropped near the edge of the hole above me. I could see dimly with the light from my grandfather's lantern, a portion of the blanket, and knew it was the body of the man they had killed lying there.

My head was swirling and I began hovering over that hole, only to be dropped back abruptly by my thoughts again. That was when I thought of becoming a rat so that I could climb up the side of that deep hole and escape. I could hear voices in my head. That had not happened before. It was as if a lot of people were talking and yet I couldn't understand what they were saying. Up until this time I could hear movements above me, but then there was total silence except for the voices in my head. My grandfather was apparently gone as was the light from his lantern and I wondered if he would ever come back. I was still afraid to cry, however, in case he was still in the vicinity. Instead I sat down and buried my head in my sweater. I was dirty and tired and wanted to die. It was dark now and there was no one to help me, not unless Papa returned as he had promised. There I found myself at the bottom of that hole with the victim's body lying above me.

During the time I was in that hole there were a lot of things I recalled. I thought about Donald and me becoming friends and exploring the woods at the edge of the pasture. I thought about us riding tricycles on warm summer days. I thought of riding on the hay baler with my uncle and Barry making a chariot for me. I thought of Easter egg hunts, and safe cozy nights with my mom and dad. Sometimes the fear would overtake me again and I would go back to being a rat scratching frantically on the sides of that freshly dug grave. I even thought about God. Where was God? Was He still flying about the pasture on Mrs. Fuller's land, or maybe He was listening to another little girl's prayers. My thoughts were racing so much that I felt I couldn't contain them.

I don't know exactly how long I stayed in the hole that night but I do know when I saw a ladder being placed at the end of it, I assumed that the nightmare was over. Little did I know that it was only just beginning. I didn't remember the walk back, nor did I remember what had happened until many years later. My life had again taken a drastic turn that night in the woods behind my grandparent's house, a course that would lead me on many dead end streets and into valleys of despair. That night, however, I was just glad to be out of the hole and on my way back to a warm cozy bed. Even the bed, where I had been afraid so many times, looked inviting. Just as I had taken a bath and crawled into bed I heard my grandmother come through the door. I could only guess that I had been in that hole about three hours. In the morning it was fortunate that I did not remember the events of the night before. The memories were tucked away neatly in my mind along with all the other secrets that could never be told.

She finally said, "Claudette, you don't fit in." Inside I gasped, and thought to myself that being slapped in the face would have been far preferable to hearing those four little words...

CHAPTER 7

Three Flights Down

The weeks and months that followed the night in the woods were ones where I experienced intense nightmares. I hated nights, even at my parent's house. On some occasions my mom would find me in my closet at 2:00 am in the morning, with a flashlight, reading. She would be furious because I had to be ready for school the next day. I would always tell her that I just wasn't sleepy, but the real reason that I didn't want to go to bed were the frequency of the nightmares. I couldn't understand why I kept hearing voices in my head. I wasn't going to tell my mother, for fear of being locked away in an asylum. I had heard stories of a family member who was a bit strange. Mama had said this aunt needed to be locked up in a padded cell. Perhaps I had taken after her. I wondered many times if this was where I might end up.

I knew that I was different from my friends. Even in a group I always felt like an outsider. It wasn't that I didn't wear beautiful clothes, because my grandmother saw to it that I had the best. To be part of the 'in group' at school you most certainly had to have nice clothes. I definitely qualified in that way, but I still didn't feel comfortable around a lot of people. I had several favorite friends, among who were, Susan the pastor's daughter and Jean, whose parents were good friends of my mom and dad's. I still thought about death a lot and my favorite pastime at the weekend was playing with my dolls.

One Saturday, late in the afternoon, I was home alone with Papa. Mama had gone to the grocery store. I never liked being with him alone, but my grandmother said she also needed to visit the hospital to check on a sick friend, and children weren't allowed there.

I was sitting on the floor, putting a new outfit on Linda, one of my dolls, when my grandfather called. I got up quickly as I was accustomed to doing. I walked through the hall and saw him standing by his bed, in his room, counting money. The two single beds were completely covered. There was not one bare spot. The stacks of bills not only covered his single bed but my grandmother's as well. I stood there gazing at the money and wondered why he didn't have it in a bank. I knew that he always had stacks of bills in his wallet but I truly had never seen this much at one time. He reached down and handed me a five dollar bill. I was used to him giving me a dollar bill every once in a while, when my grandmother would take me by his shop, but he had never given me this much before. He told me that I had earned it for keeping our secrets. My first impulse was to slap it out of his hand but I knew better than to take any action of that nature. I reached out and took the money, swallowing hard. I slowly turned around and walked back to my bedroom and lost myself in play with my dolls.

The next day, which was a Sunday, right before Training Union, I walked outside the lower building of our church, just to get some fresh air. Our group met in the basement of the church and I really hated that place. For some reason it made me feel closed in and so I had just needed to get outside for a few minutes. I looked down and saw a jagged piece of glass lying near the door. Apparently someone had broken a bottle and this piece had not been retrieved. I picked up the glass. I don't know what happened with that piece of glass in my hand, but the next thing I was aware of, was standing back in the basement near the bathroom with my left hand hurting really badly. I looked down only to find multiple cuts on my hand and there was a trail of blood leading from the hall to the bathroom. About that time one of my friends, Nancy Gail, came around the corner, saw me, and ran to get our teacher. She in turn, immediately ran upstairs to get my mom who took me home.

For the first time I felt like a criminal being interrogated. My mom and dad kept me up until five the next morning, questioning me about how those cut marks got there. I had been found out for sure. In order to conceal the truth, I said that there was a piece of glass in my purse which had cut me when I reached in to get some money. Fortunately none of the cuts were deep enough to have stitches, but they were prominent enough to show a variety of marks and other shapes on my hand.

Mother was furious. She knew there was no way that these types of cuts could possibly have happened by sticking my hand in a bag. She conceded it was possible for one, perhaps, but not twenty or thirty. I didn't know what to tell them because I had not even remembered cutting myself. I knew that I had done it before, but most of the time it was just to get some release from the pressure I was under. My dad sat and listened, not saying much. He did mention to my mom a few times that she needed to let me go to bed. He drank about a pot of coffee during this very long inquisition. I knew he was as tired as I was but my mom didn't want to let up.

I sat silent most of the time not saying much as she ranted on and on about how embarrassing this was for the family. She finally said, "Claudette, you don't fit in." Inside I gasped, and thought to myself that being slapped in the face would have been far preferable to hearing those four little words. I was already aware that I didn't fit in, but Mother had never actually said this to me before. This was just confirming to me what my grandmother had already said. I wished at that moment that the floor would have swallowed me up. I truly didn't want to live and I wished I had never been born. Just as a crystallizing event can change a person's course of life, there are also specific words which can create a core of rejection, deep bitter roots that touch the depths of the soul. It would take me many years to uproot these. I, at that time, knew nothing about the power of the Holy Spirit in my life because I didn't know Jesus. I was also very unsure of the God of the 'Pasture.'

I cried myself to sleep for what little there was left of the night. My mom didn't wake me up for school the next morning since I had very little sleep the night before. She didn't take me to the doctor either. She said there was no point because he would just tell her that I was going through a phase and that I would soon outgrow it, and she was tired of hearing him say that.

There was one thing about our family in that once an incident had happened and been talked over, it was never brought up again. I wasn't sure at that time if this was a good thing or a bad thing. I know that Mother watched me more carefully and checked on me more often when I was alone in my room. She wouldn't allow me to close my door and I was subject to a surprise inspection in the middle of the night, to make sure I wasn't in the closet with a flashlight or a piece of glass. Sometimes I would still be awake in the early morning, afraid to sleep because of the horrible nightmares that I was experiencing and could hear her tiptoe into my room to see if I was in my bed. I didn't let on that I was still awake.

It was getting near to Christmas and a Training Union Christmas party was planned. My grandmother had bought me a beautiful red plaid dress with a black ribbon belt. I kept a gauze bandage around my hand to conceal the cuts and when any of my friends mentioned it, I would always find a way to change the subject. I was actually excited about that party, and the greatest thing was that, I didn't have to spend the night with Mama and Papa that weekend. This would be the first time I had spent a weekend with my parents rather than my grandparents.

We met in the social hall on a Saturday night. Jean and Susan were there and we were laughing and talking and waiting for the refreshments to be served. There was a full program of games and activities planned for us. Even though this was a happy occasion, it was also a sad one for me because Jean, one of my best friends, was going to be moving to Florida. I was going to miss her so much. There were very few girls who I was close to, apart from Jean and Susan, and now Jean would be leaving. We decided between us that this could be her 'going away' party.

Nancy Gail, a tall heavy set girl, also in our Training Union group, came over to us. She had a book in her hand. She handed it to me and said right in front of my other two friends, "I think you need to read this." The title of the book was 'Mental Illness Is A

Family Affair'. I could feel myself blushing. I wanted to run but I didn't want to make a scene. I took the book and Susan and Jean both stared down at the book and gave Nancy Gail a dirty look. She giggled and turned around and walked off.

What transpired after the incident with the book, I never recalled, but I do remember walking up two flights of steps near the sanctuary of the church. There were no lights on there, but I could still faintly see from the lights in the basement. As I slowly walked up those steps I had one thing in mind. I had no intention of leaving this church alive. I got to the top of the stairway that led to the adult Sunday school rooms, and just stood there for a moment. I was crazy and others knew it and I had to end it all. Then without fear or any other type of emotion I deliberately lunged down those steps. I was disappointed when I found there was virtually no damage done and so climbed the stairs again. This time I was determined to do it right. The second fall apparently knocked me out and, when I regained consciousness, my back and head hurt badly. There were people standing over me and I heard Jean say, "Claudette, are you ok?"

Within minutes an ambulance arrived and took me to the hospital. I don't know how long I was in the hospital, but I remember not talking to anyone about what had happened that night. There were no broken bones but I had a concussion and a back injury which the doctor said would just take time to heal. The preacher came to the hospital and prayed for me, but all I could do was to stare up at the ceiling. I was just so sorry that I hadn't succeeded in my plan to die. I determined not to forget my decision to take my own life and so purposed in my mind that, when the time was right, I would make it happen.

It would be several months later that my mom took me to a chiropractor out of town as my back was still painful. In order for him to work on my back, I had to wear a gown with a rear opening and then stand on a table which was lowered to bring my back into a straight position. For the first few visits everything went fine and then one time without warning, while straightening me out on the examination table, he began fondling me. It was only for a brief few seconds but enough for me to know that this was wrong. The first time it happened I sat silent the whole way home. Mother asked me what was wrong but I told her nothing. One thing that I had learned in my twelve short years was that there were things you just didn't tell. I yet again had another secret for my dolls. I was glad they were there waiting for me every weekend. I knew that I could depend on them. The voices in my head were getting even stronger but that fact also had to be kept hidden from the adults in my life.

Church had become a place of solace for me and deep down there was the thought that becoming 'Queen' would certainly win my parent's approval ...

CHAPTER 8

The Coronation

Some of my friends were joining the church. I wanted to be accepted into my group of peers, so one Sunday morning I walked down the aisle during the invitation. The preacher asked me if I believed that Jesus was the Son of God. I said that I did and he welcomed me into the church. I was quite unaware at that time of the scripture in James 2:19 which says, "Thou, believest that there is one God; thou doest well: the devils also believe, and tremble." My decision to shake the preacher's hand that morning was only to keep in line with what my friends were doing. Most of them were twelve years old which was considered to be the age of accountability. I thought that maybe getting to know this God a bit better might help me to feel more positive about myself.

I tried praying to God and even joined a group of young people who memorized scripture, and participated in 'sword drills' during some of the Sunday evening services. I excelled at this and even won a few of the scripture challenges. In spite of all this memorization, the verses didn't mean a lot to me. They were only words on a page which spoke of a God that I didn't feel really cared much about me.

One of the highlights of my pre-adolescent days was my church activity. In my heart, I felt that church was a safe place. At that time there weren't a lot of places where I felt secure, but church provided me with the most positive influence, except for those Friday nights with my mom and dad which I loved.

Girl's Auxiliary was my all-time favorite program at church. There was a progression of steps you could complete, beginning with 'Maiden', and then following with 'Princess', 'Lady in Waiting', 'Queen', 'Queen with a Scepter' and 'Queen Regent'. From the onset of being told that I could become a 'Queen' in Girl's Auxiliary, I excitedly began my work to achieve that status. There was a lot of competition with the other girls to reach this goal, and as the steps progressed they became more difficult. The qualifications for becoming a 'Queen' were very detailed, requiring a lot of scripture memorization and knowledge of Paul's missionary journeys. There were three leaders who acted as examiners, quizzing us on particular steps and then awarding us either a passing grade, or the opportunity to repeat those parts which we had not done correctly. Although I had some trouble memorizing it all, because my concentration skills at that time seemed so limited, I determined that I would at least reach the title of 'Queen.' My mom encouraged me, as well as my GA leader, Mrs. Benjamin.

One very positive thing that my mom always communicated was that if you begin something you don't quit until it is completed. Even when I began piano lessons, she informed me that I would be required to continue taking music until I finished high school, but what I did with it after that time was to be my decision. It was the same thing with my steps in Girl's Auxiliary. Although she had to constantly remind me to practice the piano, she had no problem motivating me to do those GA steps, because I seemed to thrive on the competition.

The reason for my enthusiasm was probably a means of compensating for the insecurity I felt, when competing for the attention of my parents, after my sister was born. Even though I wouldn't admit it at the time, I did love my sister and found it fascinating to watch the funny things she did. The only times I had negative thoughts about her were when my grandmother would remind me that my parents didn't love me as much as they did my sister. At that time I didn't identify this as being a lie. I had been accustomed to so many mixed messages from authority figures that I didn't know what to believe. I loved my mom and dad and neither of them ever abused me in any way but those untruths, spoken by my grandmother, were ever present in my mind.

Church had become a place of solace for me, and deep down there was the thought that becoming 'Queen' would certainly win my parent's approval. Susan, the preacher's daughter had already advanced beyond 'Queen' status, and although I knew I could not get that far, I still spent long hours working on my assignments in order to reach my own goal. There was a great incentive to reach this step because the 'Queen' position earned the right to have a Coronation Service at church, including the privilege of wearing a long gown. The new queen could also choose her own 'Crown Bearer'. It was a big event and after a year of very hard work I had finally become 'Queen'. Susan had gone on to become 'Queen with a Scepter.' There was one more step which was 'Queen Regent', but none of the girls had attained this. I wasn't at all pleased that Susan was ahead of me but at least I had reached 'Queen' position.

My mother was working as a secretary for a Veterinarian in our town, who also attended our church. This man had a son who was about seven years old and my mother thought that perhaps he would like to be my 'Crown Bearer'. We talked to his parents, and they agreed to let him do this. My mother picked out a pattern, which was for a white chiffon dress with ruffles at the top, and my grandmother, who was an excellent seamstress, made it for me.

The excitement grew as the day approached for the big event. I was very nervous because I had to quote many scripture verses and also had to give a clear account of one of Paul's missionary journeys. I had mixed feelings, and my greatest fear was that of my mind going blank in front of the church. I so wanted to do it right. My only reservation, was realizing that my grandfather might be in that congregation. I secretly hoped that he wouldn't come, but knew in my heart that he would most probably want to attend. I purposed in my mind; therefore, that if he was present, I would not look in his direction that night.

Another exciting event that would happen was that two weeks after the Coronation ceremony, the girls who had reached the level of 'Queen' would be invited to attend a weekend at Limestone College.

They would actually be able to meet with Miss Marjorie Sanders who was the National Girl's Auxiliary Director. We knew a lot about her and she was such an inspiration to us all, especially on those occasions when she would visit our church to speak. She was a tall, thin lady with a soft voice and there was something about her that so intrigued me. I had mentally put her on my list of possible women to talk with about my problems, although I knew the chances of that ever happening were slim. She was a very high profile lady and I could not imagine sitting down with her and telling my secrets, even if I had the opportunity. I could, however, always fantasize about being able to share those secrets that weighed so heavily on my mind.

The culmination of all I had worked for was about to take place in the First Baptist Church in town. I, Sarah Claudette Cooper, would be walking down the aisle of my church to receive a crown. I was nervous but very excited and as the moment approached for me to walk down that aisle, followed by my Crown Bearer, I felt significant and someone of value who had accomplished something positive. This was the first time in my life that I had dared to feel this way about myself. At least for that night there would be no need for hovering, or escaping into my fantasy world. This was real and beautiful and it was happening to me. I prayed that I wouldn't trip, or forget the memory verses that had been rehearsed so many times.

As I stood on that platform in front of a crowded church and recited those verses followed by the detailed journey of Paul, I felt a calmness come over me, much the same as I had felt that summer day in the pasture behind my house. I spoke with confidence, never faltering once nor forgetting any of the scriptures. After my presentation, the young boy carrying my crown approached, and Mrs. Benjamin placed it on my head. The congregation applauded. I recalled again the story that my mother had written of the pianist who looked into the faces of his audience and heard the words of his father saying, "Well done!" For one brief moment, in that church, I had heard those words also.

After arriving home that night, my dress neatly hung and shoes placed on the rack in my closet, I settled down for a much needed rest. From the faint glow of the nightlight I could see my crown as it sat majestically on top of the dresser. I lay in my bed for a few minutes just thinking about the events of that evening. I had not felt this much satisfaction and contentment in a long time. Playing with my dolls was fun and I adored them, but this was different and even more special in that it was a Saturday night and I was not at Mama and Papa's house, but there in my own bed. I wouldn't be afraid tonight nor would I be cringing at the shuffle of evil feet as they approached my bedroom door.

Tonight was the first night that I actually felt that I had accomplished something of value. "Value, I did something of value!" I exclaimed inside, as I sat up quickly in bed. I slid out from under the covers, walked to my door and closed it so I would not be detected as I turned on the lamp. I opened up my wardrobe, the same one which had sat in our first tiny house, and in the bottom drawer near the back I found a white laced handkerchief. It was brand new and still in the box.

I went to my desk, got pen and paper, sat down and wrote these words, 'Pure and spotless may I be, until the day that I can see.' I stayed there for a while; reading those lines over and over again, then gently folded the piece of paper and placed it back in the box with the white handkerchief. This was to be my secret which I would keep concealed forever. It would be symbolic of how I wanted my life to be, in spite of how black and dirty it appeared at times. My desire was to be able to cherish every part of that night because there might not be another one like that ever again. For some reason it was very important for me to write those words. This was something that I always wanted to keep, as a reminder of the little girl who I aspired to be.

The box would not be placed in my wardrobe where my mom might discover it. I had to find a secret hideaway where it could not possibly be detected. Where would it be safe? I went to the big closet in my bedroom which wasn't used as much as my wardrobe. There I kept a lot of my games, and a few of my favorite dolls which my grandmother had finally allowed me bring to my house. She had reluctantly let them go and her reasoning was, that they now could not be carried into the 'dirty pasture'. By this time my parents and I were living back in the city, a block from town. I had Ann, Susie, and the three faced doll with me. Miss Daffney Dupont, however, still resided on the top shelf of the hall closet, at my grandparent's house, as well as Faye, Terri Lee, Linda, and Baby Linda.

I stood looking into the open closet for a few minutes surveying any suitable place to hide my treasure. "Perfect!" I managed to stifle a squeal of delight, as I found just the right spot for my secret box, handkerchief, and note. There was a small door with a latch, at one end of the closet. I carefully lifted the latch and knew that I had found the ideal location. There was a ledge above the door and as I placed the box on to it, carefully sliding it to one side, I realized that it was then totally out of view and that I had found a unique hiding place. With a great sense of relief, I affectionately rubbed the top of the box one last time, and closed the small door and latched it back.

This was the first secret which was truly mine, not one that I had been threatened into keeping. It was also a good and pure secret, one which I would be able to think about and draw strength from when needed. This time there was to be no applause, except for the words that kept ringing through my head. For the second time in one night, I could again hear the words, "Well done." I smiled to myself as I crawled back into bed.

… I knew what the word adopted meant. I pretended not to hear but her answers rang out loud and clear…

CHAPTER 9

Foundations Rocked

E ven though I was extremely excited about my trip to Limestone College, there was an incident which occurred shortly before we were supposed to leave, which confused and perplexed me more than I had ever been in the past. It was arranged for me to spend an afternoon with another aunt who lived within walking distance of my grandparent's house. She was married to my grandmother's brother, whose name was Barney, but who we nicknamed Bombie. There was a very unusual setup in the vicinity where I spent most weekends, as most of our immediate family lived within walking distance of each other, that is all but my parents, who lived about eight miles from them in the small historic town of Abbeville. Aunt Grace who was my grandmother's sister, her husband nicknamed MB and my cousin Barry, lived about an eighth of a mile south of my grandparent's house but Aunt Ruth and Bombie lived just east of them on a hill near the main highway leading into town.

Aunt Ruth was a tall thin lady with bright red hair and was referred to as the 'backbone' of our family. I wasn't one to ask what phrases meant, although we were all aware of how strong willed she was, and the fact that if anyone had a particular problem, Aunt Ruth would be the one with the answer. She would also give advice whether she had been asked or not. This would sometimes irritate my grandmother but then most things did. Aunt Ruth's brother was my dad's father, who had died many years earlier. She had introduced my mom and dad to each other when my mom was attending college, and living with her for awhile. I had been told that she would have still been part of the family, even if Bombie had not married her, since her brother was my father's dad. As it all seemed a bit complex to me, I dismissed it from my mind, a safeguard I often practiced.

On this particular day, Aunt Ruth and I were going to do some 'girl' things together. My grandmother had asked her to take me on a shopping trip, since she herself was going to be canning vegetables and couldn't leave her stove. I needed a few new clothes to take on my weekend conference and this was a good opportunity to get them. We intended to set out early in the morning to be there when the stores opened. It took me approximately four minutes to walk to Aunt Ruth's house, which was on the adjoining land to my grandparent's seventy two acres. I was used to long shopping trips with my grandmother and also the resulting argument if I disagreed with what she felt I should purchase. I was happy on this occasion that I didn't have to go with my grandmother, and hoped that I might have some leeway in my choices.

Aunt Ruth was ready when I arrived, as she prided herself in her punctuality. She was a sought after executive secretary and very much a perfectionist, but not to the extent that my grandmother was, in maintaining an immaculate house. I did see her, however, as someone who had it all together when it came to knowing just about everything. She thanked me for being on time and we immediately left on our shopping trip to town. There were times that I felt intimidated by Aunt Ruth. I think it was because of her directness and the fact that she spent a lot more time with Barry than she did with me. I felt a bit jealous of their relationship much like I did with my sister and parents.

My aunt wasn't one to waste a lot of time selecting clothes and so quickly suggested two really nice outfits which even I liked. We purchased them at one of the nicest shops in town and within thirty minutes were ready to run some other errands which were on Aunt Ruth's list. Her next one was to take the car to the service station and have the oil changed. While there the owner approached her and asked, "Whose little girl is this?" My aunt replied with the stunning remark, "This is Vivian and BJ Cooper's adopted daughter, Claudette."

I stood there not saying a word, but even though there were a lot of things I didn't understand in life, I knew what the word adopted meant. I pretended not to hear but her answer rang out loud and clear. Had I been lied to all those years? Was my mother not really my mother and was that what they had meant about my dad not being my biological father? Even though my first impulse was to cry, I had learned many times that crying wasn't what young girls did. I stood shyly on one side while my aunt talked to the owner.

I didn't have a lot to say on the way home either but I was determined to get some answers about that adoption issue. When we arrived back home, I walked straight into the kitchen and fired a point blank question at my grandmother, asking her if I was adopted. Normally I would have asked my mom first but this was a Saturday and I wouldn't be seeing her until church on Sunday, and I wasn't going to wait that long. Mama explained to me that my mom had been married to my real father, whom I didn't know, but they had divorced before I was born. She added that the man who I now called daddy had adopted me so that I could legally have the name Cooper. She went on to explain that she did not like my real father and that he had agreed to give up his parental rights for a price. "He sold you Claudette", she related with great pleasure.

I began thinking about my uncle selling his cows and later finding out that my grandfather had sold Maude also, but wanted me to believe that he had killed her. All I could think of at that moment was that you sold animals, not people. It would also be many years later that I would find out that this accusation regarding my real father wasn't true. He had in fact tried many times to see me, but all his attempts had been to no avail, because my grandmother wouldn't permit that to happen and had manipulated my mother into agreeing never to allow him to see me.

My grandmother talked on and on about a man I had never known but who was my real father, and I realized that he was out there somewhere. I fantasized that perhaps he would be a hero or a knight in shining armor and come to rescue me, so that I would not have those long weekends with my grandparents. Perhaps I would be able to visit him on weekends instead of them. Those plans were thwarted by the realization that he lived in another state, had remarried and had more children of his own. I even found out that I had a half sister and brother whom I had never met. I asked my grandmother what state he lived in but she refused to tell me. She commented that I was better off never seeing him and besides he had a new family which I was not a part of. I remember hearing those words many times in regard to my mom, dad and sister Bonnie and so my rejection was reinforced.

One thing that was evident; my grandmother obviously hated my real father, and said she had encouraged my mother in the divorce. She said that if my mom had listened to her in the first place, she would never have married him. She reminded me again of how much she and Papa loved me and that there was no one else who would love me as much as they did, or do the things for me that they had done. She used a few choice swear words that day, similar to those which my grandfather used when he was angry. This was the first time I had ever heard her say a curse word and I was well aware of the anger she felt concerning my real dad. My grandmother reminded me that the man that my mother was now married to, was my stepfather, and then again reminded me of her and Papa's allegiance to me.

I almost wished the question hadn't been asked about adoption and, at this point, I definitely did not want to hear anymore. My feeling of insecurity led me to the hall closet to get my dolls. There were many things that I needed to talk to them about that day. In the midst of all the instability in my life the dolls were always there waiting. I sat on the floor of my bedroom with tears running down my face, as my grandmother continued her canning, oblivious to the turmoil she had created within me.

I also talked to God that day asking him to please help me find my daddy, and if I was successful then to make it possible that I could go to visit him and get to know my brother and sister. This thought gave me a faint glimmer of hope, that perhaps God would hear my prayers and make all the wrong things right again. I wondered as I sat on the floor with my 'secret-keeping friends' why people didn't get along, why people hated others, why people divorced, why there were times that I couldn't remember what happened the day before, and most of all why some adults hurt children and especially those who were in their care.

My love for my stepfather was great and I had really known no other father, and so I couldn't stand the thought of hurting his feelings by asking to see my real dad. It was a few days later that my mom and dad did talk to me about my real father, Jack. They told me that if I ever wanted to visit him, they would take me. I assumed that my grandmother had related to them what I had asked that day, when I had challenged her. Still I said little in reply, but continued later with my comfort activity of sharing concerns with my dolls.

I ran to her and grabbed her with such a force that I even surprised myself, and desperately clung to her…

CHAPTER 10

Queen's Court

W e had arrived at one of my most exciting weekends ever. The trip to Limestone College was one of constant chatter, singing songs and telling jokes. Susan and I sat together in the van and we talked about how much fun our weekend was going to be, and the fact that we would be able to see Miss Marjorie Sanders. She was to be speaking at our evening meeting and there would also be girls from all over the state for the 'Queen's Court' weekend. There were six in our group and although I wasn't particularly happy about the fact that Nancy Gayle was with us, she was entitled to be there as she had also reached 'Queen' status. I intended to make sure that I stayed clear of her, however, especially after the incident where she had given me the book on mental illness.

Just after five o'clock, our white van pulled up on the circular driveway of the main building at the college, and we were all anxious to get out and find our rooms. There would be a rally early in the afternoon, followed by dinner and then Miss Sanders would be speaking. After the meeting we would be having refreshments and the next day was going to be packed with all types of activities. A banquet was planned for the Saturday evening followed by a trip to the big indoor swimming pool. Although I had gained a few unwanted pounds, Aunt Ruth and I were able to find a flattering swim suit, which I felt comfortable in along with a few other nice items of casual wear, now packed neatly in my brown suitcase.

That night as we sat and listened to Miss Sanders, I literally held on to each word that she said. I thought she was an amazing woman in every way. She had a passion about her that impressed me and I thought how wonderful it would be to be like her one day. She told us of the mission trips she had made and I was especially intrigued with her stories of Africa and the desire to establish a Girl's Auxiliary there among the African children. She said that God might even call one of us to go there someday. I wondered how that would be, to actually sit among the tribal children and talk with them, in much the same way I had with my friends 'Cootie' and 'Booger Ball'.

Suddenly I felt sick, my heart began to pound. I for some reason felt sad, and the more I tried to concentrate on what Miss Sanders was saying, the more my thoughts seemed to race into the woods where I had transported myself so many times. It felt as if something was squeezing me tightly and I couldn't breathe. It was much the same sensation that I had experienced a few times when I had fallen off my swing, and the wind was knocked out of me. I fidgeted in my seat. Susan nudged me and asked if everything was alright. I told her I was fine but that wasn't the case at all. I kept thinking about my three-faced doll, lying peacefully in imaginary death repose, as she had done on many occasions when we held funerals for her. I realized my thoughts were out of control and knew I had to somehow bring them into line.

"Stop this!" I commanded myself inwardly, not taking my eyes off Miss Sanders. I began to breathe a bit slower then and within a few minutes felt like I was in control again. I definitely didn't want any incidents spoiling my weekend away. Mother had already been uneasy about me going on that retreat and cautioned me that she wouldn't be at all pleased if she had to be contacted concerning any crisis that might arise. Her concern for me had grown whenever I was away from home, especially after my fall down the flight of stairs at the Training Union Christmas Party.

It had taken a lot of convincing to get my mom to allow me to go on this weekend retreat. I think Mrs. Benjamin; the pastor's wife had assured her that Susan would keep an eye on me and that it would be good for me to attend. I didn't know how much mother shared with any of her friends about the problems she had with me from time to time, but I was told had it not been for Mrs. Benjamin, then I wouldn't be going at all. I received more than one warning from my mom regarding my behavior before we left for our weekend away.

Mother had told me that I needed to act responsibly and that cutting or any other self abusive activity was not a way of building trust. She had become concerned about allowing me to leave the house, not knowing when she would get a call from the hospital saying I had been injured or cut. It had happened far too many times for her not to worry.

I didn't want mother to be anxious and was going to do everything in my power to see that nothing happened to give her any concern. In bed that night I was still thinking about the virtues of Miss Sanders. There was something about that lady which made me think of God. She seemed to exude an excitement and when she said the name Jesus, a peace would come over me. Those kinds of emotions didn't happen very often in my life, so when they did it was very refreshing. I went to sleep that night thinking happy thoughts, anticipating the next day's activities.

The following day was filled with classes and a lot of new things to learn. We had a choice between classes on missions, or going to prepare for higher steps in Girl's Auxiliary. I took the mission class because I felt they might again talk about Africa. I was really intrigued with that country and especially the idea of spending more time with black friends like I had at home. Even though my grandmother, grandfather and uncles all hated the black race, I felt there was something about them that was very sincere and loyal. At my grandparent's house when Aunt Mary and her children had to wait until we had our dinner before they were given anything to eat, she never seemed insulted. Sometimes 'Cootie' and 'Booger Ball' would be hungry and my mom would slip them a biscuit or piece of chicken to tide them over until my grandmother would allow them to eat their meal.

Aunt Mary would sometimes tell us Bible stories when she came to iron. We would sit on the floor as she sprayed the clothes with water from a soda bottle, which had a sprinkler on the end, and rattle on for hours with stories like Jonah being swallowed by the whale and she also sung us some Negro spirituals. We loved to hear Aunt

Mary sing and when she did it came from her heart. I thought that Jonah being trapped in a fish's belly couldn't be much worse than some of the things that had happened to me, but then the concept of being swallowed by a fish really wasn't my idea of a fun day either.

Back to Queen's College; however, this was a special day and there I was with the other girls who had reached the level of 'Queen'. We were all excited about the big banquet which would be held in just a few hours. We went back to our rooms to rest awhile after the classes and then got dressed for the night's event. I had thought about washing my hair but then decided to leave it as I knew that we would later be going swimming and it seemed to look present-able enough for the evening. Having naturally curly hair did have its advantages at times like that.

The hour finally arrived when we all met in the huge dining room of the college. The tables were decorated beautifully with flowers and candles. We each had a personal place name card and I felt really special. I thought about the story in the Bible of the 'Marriage Supper of the Lamb' and wondered if there might be a possibility that I would be among the ones who would be invited to attend, but then as bad as I felt I was at times, it made me not sure.

We all took our seats and I was surprised to find that we weren't together with those we already knew. This made me feel a bit uncom-fortable, but we were told that this was a good way for us to meet some of the other girls who had attended. This arrangement made me uneasy because I was not secure in being around people that I didn't know. Susan was sitting at the table directly behind me and Nancy Gayle was quite a distance away so that did make me feel a little more relaxed. Just to be out of her gaze and scrutinizing stare was a relief and so made up for the lack of friends around me.

It would have been an honor to have been at the same table as Miss Sanders although I realized that probably wasn't going to happen. She sat in the upper part of the dining room with all the other leaders and weekend personnel, but our table was positioned in such a way that I could still see her. She smiled all the time. I wondered how it would feel to be that happy, but in my mind there was always a shadowy cloud which seemed to drown out the happi-ness that I so desired to have. But for that night I was a Queen in

Girl's Auxiliary and that was good enough for me. I just wished those moments would last forever.

The dinner was baked chicken, steaming vegetables and rice and broccoli casserole with extra cheese sprinkled on top. I tried to remember all my rules of etiquette which Mama had so skillfully taught me. I tried not to think of the incident when she told me that if I touched a utensil on the table before the appointed time, at dinner, then I would start shaking and never stop. I always thought of it whenever I picked up a spoon or fork and wondered if the shaking could possibly happen at other times as well.

We had strawberry shortcake for dessert and as we finished our meal, Miss Sanders again got up to speak. She talked about our achievements and how God was pleased with all that we had done to reach our goals. She gave an inspiring message and even added a few things that my mother had taught me as well. One point that she emphasized was never to quit, no matter what the situations were or how tempted we might be to do so. I could identify with what she was saying because I had desperately wanted to quit many times, and even to give up on life itself. I thought about my deliberate fall down the stairs that past December. Perhaps this weekend could mark a new beginning for me, although there were nagging thoughts of having to go back home with the subsequent weekend visits to my grandparent's house. I determined that I would not allow myself to think of such things on that special night. I wanted to take in every word that Miss Sanders was saying because I felt the benefits of that evening may have to last me a long time.

Finally the meal and message ended and we planned to go back to our rooms and put on swim suits for a couple of hours of fun in the pool. The banquet had unfortunately finished sooner than I wanted it to, especially after Miss Sanders had spoken, but on the other hand I did enjoy swimming and that was to be our last night there. We excitedly went to get ready to go to the pool and those of us who did not want to get our hair wet, grabbed swim caps.

There was a large pool at the college and by the time Susan and I and a few of the other girls from our group had arrived, many others were already happily splashing in the water. There was much laughter there that bounced off the walls with a resounding echo. I definitely was not one who just jumped in a pool without checking out the water first. Even though I considered myself to be a good swimmer I always used caution, especially in new surroundings. I carefully took off my cover-up and placed it with my towel on one of the chairs nearby. I sat on the side of the pool at first and had the idea of easing myself into the water. Susan and some of the other girls were already in the pool and they urged me to get in. I sat there for a while, pondering on the fact that I was the only one not in the water so, after about five minutes, decided to join the rest.

The water felt great. It was my first time in an indoor pool and seemed to be very relaxing. That was a perfect ending to a great day. Everyone including myself was having a great time until suddenly I had a flashback of me in the bathtub at my grandparent's house. I could almost hear my grandfather saying, "Hurry up and finish your bath and Papa will take you to the shop." At that exact moment I began screaming, not just a scream like someone might do in playful excitement, but a blood curdling one which I could not seem to stop. Susan made her way over to me and grabbed me by the arm and that was the last thing I recalled. To this day I cannot remember what happened after the incident in the pool.

The next thing that I do remember was running along the corridors of a darkened hallway that night, calling out Miss Sander's name. My next action would probably have been to start knocking on doors to find her because at that time she was the only person I could remember. Near the end of the hallway a lady stepped out of her room and I recognized it to be Miss Sanders. I ran to her and grabbed her with such a force that I even surprised myself, and desperately clung to her. She tried to calm me down but I was crying uncontrollably and she stood there in the hall embracing me and asking me how she could help. All I could do was cry. After I had calmed down a bit she led me into her room.

We sat on her bed and she talked to me for awhile and the strange thing about it was, at that time, I couldn't even remember my name. I felt that I was in a strange place in some kind of time-warp and the only person I knew was Miss Sanders. She was very kind as she gently patted me on the shoulder. She comforted me by saying that God would take away all of my fears. I kept telling her that I couldn't remember what had happened or why I was crying. She explained to me that I may have had a panic attack in the pool and the college nurse had taken me back to my room and had agreed to check on me in a few hours. The nurse had come by to tell Miss Sanders later on that night that I was sleeping, as she apparently already knew about the incident.

Miss Sanders said that she would like for me to stay in the nurse's room for the rest of the night and implied that things would look a lot brighter in the morning. She kept reassuring me that everything would be fine. She also asked me if there was anything I needed to talk to her about, but nothing would come to mind. I just kept telling her I was afraid and was sorry for waking her up. She looked at me with very kind, understanding eyes and said that she was there for me and God was as well.

She walked with me back up the hall and spoke with the nurse whose room was not too far from hers. The nurse invited me in and she told me we could bunk together for the rest of the night. There were two single beds as in all the dorm rooms and she told me that she would get me an extra blanket as I was shivering very badly at the time. I had my pajamas on but no robe. The nurse got another blanket and with much care tucked it around me after I settled into bed. I was very tired, and mentally exhausted, feeling as if I had run a marathon. "You don't mind if I pray do you?" she inquired. "No, I don't mind," I answered as I tried to choke back the tears.

That nurse probably never realized what an impact she would have on my life in coming days, as there were occasions when I needed to recall the words of her very sincere prayer on that particular night at Limestone College. It went something like this, "Dear Father, I don't know what is troubling this young lady tonight but You do, and I am asking You to help her to deal with whatever problems she is having. I ask You to touch her right now and take away her fear. Keep her in Your hands, Lord, and guide her life in the days to come. Be her comforter in times of trouble and may she be made and molded into the image of Your dear Son. In Jesus name, Amen."

I drifted off to sleep, and, as troubled as I was, could almost feel the touch of angel wings. Years later I would attempt to get in touch with the nurse whose prayer and concern had reached me in such a powerful way that night. Although I would never to be able to locate and thank her, I now know that the 'God of the Pasture' had again come by to visit me at Queen's Court.

My strongholds were being built brick by brick and the lies, innu-endoes and negativity were the 'construction workers'...

CHAPTER 11

A Shocking Revelation

The following morning I felt very embarrassed being brought back to the room by the school nurse. My first task of the day was to convince Susan that there was no need to tell my mom what had happened the night before. I remembered mother's warnings before my trip to make sure I acted responsibly, and screaming in the middle of a crowded pool would not have been on her list of 'to do' things at Queen's College weekend. I knew that my strange behavior was not something that I had planned to happen but getting this fact across to friends and family wouldn't be easy to communicate. In reality I had no memory of what had transpired after the initial panic attack in the pool, and so wouldn't have been able to explain myself anyway.

When I awoke the next morning I felt disorientated and very confused about the previous night's happening. The first thing was to check my arms for any signs of cuts and was relieved to find none, as I was fairly sure there would be an inspection when I arrived home. There was always the possibility that even if Susan didn't tell, someone else would. A few of the girls in the rear of the van giggled on the way back home, remarking about my unique way of getting attention. I pretended not to hear them and just stared out of the window.

Mrs. Elliot, one of our GA leaders, who was driving the van, was preoccupied and didn't seem to take notice. I wondered what she knew and, depending on what she had been told the night before, if she too might mention it to my mom. She had asked me how I was feeling when we got into the van and I told her everything was fine. That would have been the perfect opportunity to swear her to secrecy but, from past experiences, I knew that you could not control what adults did to you and so didn't even try to influence her. I was just going to have to take my chances and hope that my mom would be happy to see me back home safe and sound.

At that time I didn't feel very sound of mind. My head hurt terribly and the voices had returned. The banquet night seemed like a dream from some way back but in my mind I could still hear the prayers of the nurse who had prayed for me the night before, which gave me a bit more hope.

My mom was waiting for me when the van pulled up at the church. She gave me a hug as the other girls were getting their suit-cases off the van, and I hurriedly placed my things in the car. I knew the moment that Mrs. Elliot motioned for my mom to come over that I was in trouble. I couldn't hear what they were saying but I knew that wasn't a good sign. Mother looked over toward me once but I couldn't detect if it was a stern look or not. I went ahead and got in the car to wait. There wasn't anywhere else to go but I felt that a lecture might be on the way and so sat there in anticipation, waiting for the onslaught.

Surprisingly, there were no comments or criticisms as I had expected. Maybe my mom decided to practice some reverse psychology, but whatever the reason, the incident at the college wasn't mentioned and I certainly had no intention of bringing it up. Secrets weren't anything new to me so I surmised that maybe this time, she was keeping the knowledge of what had happened to me the previous weekend tucked away in her own 'personal wardrobe'. I had an idea that she knew about it but, because of frustration with past issues, was reluctant to discuss anything related further with me. For some reason, unknown to me, the incident was never brought up in conversation again.

The next few months were a blur to me following the events at 'Queen's Court.' I continued my hatred of weekend visits to my grandparent's house but knew that resisting them would only place more pressure on my mom. The control that my grandmother had over her was immense and she seemed to always crumble with her mother's confrontations. Most of their arguments were about me spending time in the country but my grandmother always won. Saturday nights were spent watching TV and especially 'Lawrence Welk'. I didn't particularly like that program, mainly because it was one of my grandfather's favorites. It had become one of my all-time hated programs. I was still required to sit and watch it during family time even though I didn't like to. It would be then that my mind would wander to other places. My acquired ability to disassociate was helpful in any situation that I found to be unpleasant.

One November weekend, while at my grandparent's house, the phone rang and it was a friend of Mama's. I was in the kitchen getting something to drink and I could hear her inquire, "He's dead?" She was in the hall sitting at the small antique telephone table and I peeped around the refrigerator. She waved her hand, motioning me to leave. I went as far as I could but not so far that I couldn't hear what was being said. "I'll call Vivian and tell her." "All I can say is good riddance." When she had finished that call, she immediately called my mom. I could still hear her as she repeated, "Jack's dead, Vivian, and he killed himself." I felt as if time had stood still. Jack was my real father, whom I had never met.

How could she say such horrible things about my father? This couldn't be happening. I had hopes of meeting him one day with the possibility that he might take me to the zoo and other places that real dads took their children. After my grandmother told me he had married again with more children of his own, I never gave up the idea that he might possibly also accept me once more as his own child. Even though I loved my stepfather, a large portion of my hope was in the fact that maybe one day my birth father would come to rescue me. I fully believed, as my grandmother had reminded me so many times, that my mom, dad and Bonnie were a complete family without me and I sat on the sidelines of just not knowing who my real family was.

After my grandmother got off the phone she came to find me. By that time I had gone into the den so she wouldn't think I was eaves-dropping. She stood in the door-way and in the same matter of fact way that you would say, "Claudette, would you like a glass of tea," she said with no expression, "Your real father Jack is dead." She then walked out of the room and began rattling pans in the kitchen preparing the evening meal. I literally ran out of the house, past the barn, into the woods as fast as I could, through briers, broken limbs and past our pet cemetery where all our beloved pets were buried. From there I stumbled blindly on into the heart of the woods which at times were my place of escape, but stopped short of the clearing. That held memories, now erased, of the horrible event when I had spent three hours in a freshly dug grave one autumn night. There I stood screaming into nothingness, as at that distance it would have been impossible for anything to hear me except the squirrels or wandering deer. How long I stood there screaming I am not sure but my voice became very hoarse. Then I just sat on the ground and cried until I could cry no more.

It was getting dark and I don't know how long I had been in the woods but did hope that I could find my way back to the house. There were seventy-two acres of Papa's land and to get lost there on a cold night would be very dangerous. I only had a sweater on and was chilled to the bone by the time I could once more see the back of the barn. My grandmother was standing on the back porch when I walked up to the house. She didn't mention the fact that I had gone missing or that my eyes were swollen from crying and I knew that I had to keep my emotions to myself. There was little said at dinner that night and my father's death was never mentioned.

When I went home the next day my mom sat me down and told me again about my father's death. I didn't question her about the fact that my grandmother had said he had taken his own life, although I could certainly identify with the feeling of not wanting to live. Mother said that I was welcome to go the funeral, which was going to be at the local funeral home. He had lived out of state but because his family came from Abbeville, they would be having the funeral in town. From the depths of my soul I wanted to attend but there was the fear that I might hurt my stepfather's feelings, and didn't want to take the chance of perhaps causing him to pull away from me, more than I thought he had already done, since the birth of my sister.

One thing that I discovered many years later was the fact that when a person believes a lie, they are actually making a covenant agreement with that lie and circumstances which happen after that often reinforce those negative concepts that the person might have developed. My strongholds were being built brick by brick and the lies, innuendoes and negativity were the 'construction workers'.

Although I didn't attend my father's funeral in person, I was there in spirit, and when I found out that Betty Goin, my Junior Choir Director had sung at his funeral, I asked her many questions about it and if she had seen his children and what they looked like. I realized that they were my half brother and sister and if I had also attended the funeral I could at least have met them. I didn't even know what state they lived in so a chance of getting in touch with them in the future seemed unlikely. *

I wanted to talk in more detail to my mom about my real dad in the days that followed, but the words just wouldn't come out. Stuffing my emotions down had become a way of life and although this was the first real death in my family that I could recall, it hurt a lot because I had thought that there would be a time when I would get to meet my father in spite of what my grandmother had said. That hope had always been present in my mind. His death had crushed those dreams of meeting him and giving him a hug and kiss on the cheek. He now rested in a cemetery in Abbeville. One day I would ask my mom to take me there.

*(Contact was made later and I was privileged to meet both my brother and my sister who have since become very much a part of my life)

He chanted some sort of incantation which I didn't understand. "It is done", he said without remorse...

CHAPTER 12

The Covenant

My ability to escape pain became my focus especially on weekends. I was never far away from the watchful eye of my grandfather during my visits. His anger had accelerated to the degree that I was fearful of what he might do to harm me and my grandmother during the times when he was drunk. I never knew whether he drank during the week or not, but it was evident that at the weekends he spent a large portion of his time in the barn where he kept an endless supply of bottles. He had warned me many times not to tell my mom anything that went on while I was there, and that if I did that he would kill my grandmother. I believed him. He had threatened to do it many times. I hated it when they argued, but even though my grandmother was a very strong willed woman, she always backed down. She never pushed him, from what I could tell, past a certain point. I knew that she had to be as frightened of him as I was.

This knowledge gave me a compassion for her and I did feel that she loved me even if she could get very upset when I spilled something on the floor, or didn't put my dolls away when asked. Deep down I loved her too, although I really wanted her to be in agreement with me about staying home at weekends rather than coming to visit. There had to be a way to convince my mom that I didn't want to leave them every Saturday, but there seemed to be no solution. The upcoming months would see my fear increase to the degree that self abuse was happening more frequently and more intensely.

The dark side of life only got darker as my grandfather's involvement with the KKK increased. Their philosophy of claiming each drop of blood shed by Jesus Christ was a sacrifice for the white race only, was planted deeply into my subconscious, and I was often tied to a tree to watch horrendous acts of the Klan. This was done specifically to instill fear in me so that I would never tell the secrets, and to warn me of the consequences if I did. On one occasion my beloved friend 'Cootie' was tied to another tree as the Klan spouted off their allegiance to their very misguided cause. She was tied, not where I could see her but at a tree directly behind me, where she could view what was going on as well.

One time she cried out, "Claudette, where you at?" "I's Cootie and I needs help." I sat there on that particular night as my grandmother had to work second shift at her plant. My arms and wrists were bound, but I cried more for Cootie than I did myself. She had been born into the black race and didn't have a choice of what color her skin was. It was at those times that deep in my 'hovering' mind I prayed to the 'God of the Pasture' that one day children like Cootie would be loved and accepted by all. My uncle would often declare in anger that black people didn't have a soul. Everything within me rejected that idea and my love for the black race originated during an era when racial prejudice was so rampant.

Cootie and I made a pact that we would never tell what had happened because we feared for the safety of her mother, our Aunt Mary, and her father. They both worked on the property owned by Doc Durham, a self-made millionaire, who owed his success to a tonic called Vim Herb which he manufactured and sold. His summer home was situated across the road from Aunt Mary's house. We had no reason to believe that he was ever a part of the Klan. His kindness for the black people was evident and he would not have tolerated anything like we had experienced. Cootie was unfortunate enough to have been at my grandparent's house playing with me on the night of our ordeal in the woods. My grandfather insisted on her accompanying us and even though I kept whispering to her that she should go home, we were both taken into the woods under duress.

I had been, however, fortunate enough to be able to hide the memories of this event in an area in my mind that was beyond the usual 'hiding place', where I had stopped short of when disassociating. By then it was necessary to go past that foreboding place, my only means of survival. I wondered if Cootie had a hiding place in her mind also. After that night in the woods when both of us were tied to trees, neither of us brought up the incident again, that is, not after the initial pact that we had made. If she had, I probably would not have recalled what had happened. I was able by then, to completely block out the terrors that had occurred. It was the only thing that I felt proficient in doing. It was a dark world and I was an unwilling participant.

The fruits of such encounters in the woods continued to build huge walls and my defense mechanisms were growing stronger each day. My mind could leave my body at will, but at the time I didn't know why that was happening. I would just come back into awareness with cuts and scrapes on different parts of my body, not realizing how they got there. My wandering mind seemed to have become my greatest asset.

One Saturday afternoon while my grandmother was visiting my Aunt Grace, I was left alone in the house with my grandfather, something I always hated. Mama said she wouldn't be gone long but her visits to Aunt Grace's house were usually for at least an hour. My grandfather walked to the door of my bedroom and asked me to come into the living room. He pointed to the Grandfather Clock sitting on the beautiful mantel with its crown molding. His voice was stern and he never took his eyes off of me as he said, "Claudette, as long as this clock ticks and even when it stops, and even if I die, you will never be rid of me." He continued, "Our secrets will live on and you can never tell them to anyone. You are tied to me by these secrets." He reached in his pocket and pulled out a knife. "Hold out your hand," he demanded. "No, Papa don't!" I cried out in desperation. He reached out and took my hand, grabbed one of my fingers and nicked it, enough to draw blood. Then he did the same to his finger and pressed them together. He chanted some sort of incantation which I didn't understand. "It is done", he said without remorse. "Now go wash your hands and dry the tears as well, before Mama gets back."

I practically ran to the bathroom and quickly closed the door. I know my face must have been white. I felt as if the prick on my finger had made all the blood drain from it. I heard Papa again call me from the living room. He was standing by the fireplace and when I walked back in, he was standing there holding a newspaper. He made an odd statement, which I wouldn't understand until years later when the memories of that Saturday returned. "Don't ever touch this clock," he warned. "I am the only one who touches this clock and winds it." "Now go back to playing with your stupid dolls. You are thirteen years old and too big to play with dolls," he taunted. I turned around and went immediately to my room, shutting the door. If my grandfather had come to my door and eavesdropped he would have heard whispers that day as I related more secrets to my 'special friends', who I knew would never tell.

I had just drifted off to sleep when I was awakened by the sound of gunfire. I sat up in bed startled and was afraid to move…

CHAPTER 13

Horror Revisited

My grandmother was a superstitious woman and I found great delight in opening an umbrella in the house just to watch her reaction. I was a teenager by then and everyone knew that teenagers rebelled. My prank of putting an umbrella over my head and boldly marching into the 'den' while my grandmother was crocheting was considered a horrendous crime by her, but was the only way I had at that time of showing some independence. It was rather humorous to watch her throw her handiwork to one side and chase me as I ran through the kitchen into the hall giggling and saying, "Catch me if you can." She didn't find it at all funny. When she finally caught up with me I would get a lecture on how dangerous this was in terms of what would happen to me for testing the 'gods'. She would then mark an imaginary 'x' at the spot where she had retrieved the umbrella, with a warning that if it happened again I would be sent to bed without dinner.

Mama planted garlic around all the corners of the house and when I asked her why she said very emphatically, "Claudette, they keep the evil spirits away." I knew this wasn't working because my grandfather was still there. I had never thought about him being a spirit but I did see the evil things which he did, and the presence of darkness was something I was very aware of when he was around. It would be many years later before the full impact of all that had taken place would hit me. When it came, it was with such force that, had anyone told me what would transpire, I would not have comprehended it at that particular time. I was just glad that I had found a way to escape the horrors as they happened.

My defense mechanism of mentally leaving my body had been skillfully set in place. Thoughts could lead me to any one of a number of rooms. One jolt of anything unpleasant could send me there. I had three special rooms, one which I used at annoying times, called the 'waiting place', the 'hiding place' for those the times when my grandfather was abusive and drunk, and 'past the hiding place' for those intense times in the woods. One of my special rooms was needed when, within that month on a Saturday afternoon, I opened the door of the hall closet to discover that my dolls were gone. I stood there for a moment, just thinking, "Mama must have...nooo, "I argued with myself, "It must have been Papa, because he called my dolls stupid." I had much the same feeling as that day I walked to the barn and found Maude was gone, the shock of yet another unexpected happening and loss.

At the time my grandfather was outside and my grandmother was sitting in her rocking chair looking at some recipes. She was a good cook, there was no denying that. She spent a lot of time finding just the right recipe and everything she cooked was to perfection. Right then I wasn't concerned about the night's entrée, I just needed to know what had happened to the dolls. My heart was beating so fast that I actually felt dizzy. I finally gathered my courage and inquired," Mama, where are my dolls?"

Mama looked up from what she was doing and replied, "Claudette! You are fourteen and too old to play with dolls, so your mother gave them away to Bonnie Jean." I know that I showed an expression of horror and total disbelief as if what she was saying hadn't really sunk in, I returned to the hall closet to see if somehow I had been mistaken and that it was all a dream, but it wasn't. The dolls were definitely gone. All my special friends had been stolen right out of the hall closet. I stood there for a few more minutes just looking at the empty shelves which once held my dearest friends. The metal trunks with elaborate wardrobes had been replaced with a large crochet basket and tool box. I quickly ran back into the living room and immediately asked my grandmother if she would take me home. She tried to comfort me by implying that I would find another interest instead of playing with dolls. She even offered to teach me to crochet. That gave me no comfort at all to think that crocheting could possibly take the place of my doll 'confidantes'.

All those dolls were mine. My grandmother had bought them for me. I had shared all of my secrets with them. They had never been Bonnie's dolls. I begged Mama to take me home that night but she refused. I slowly and sadly walked out of the living room and back into my bedroom. There at the end of my bed, partially hidden, I noticed Ann, Susie and the three faced doll. I carefully placed them on the right side of my bed where they wouldn't be detected. I was glad that they had not been in the closet with the others. I closed the door of my bedroom and cried for hours. Then in my mind I went 'past the hiding place', that special area that had been created for crisis situations such as I then found myself in. When my grandmother called me for dinner that evening I pretended to be asleep. I really had no desire for food. I only wanted my family of dolls back.

When I arrived home the next day I went straight to my mom to see if I could get the other dolls back. She, just like Mama, told me that my doll playing days were over. She explained that little girls played with dolls, not teenagers, and it was time for me to move forward in my life. She also mentioned the fact that I couldn't continue to live in a fantasy world. She said one day I would understand why she had taken that action, but I knew it wasn't fantasy. It was real and my dolls were gone, all but the three that I had managed to hide at my grandparent's house.

I usually carried my three favorite ones back home on a Sunday afternoon, but on that occasion I had not done so as I was feeling very insecure and fearful about losing them as well. I was surprised that my mom didn't question me about the three that weren't in the closet, although I had so many dolls perhaps she just hadn't noticed. At that point I didn't even want to go into my sister's room to see the missing dolls, at least while my mom and dad were anywhere around. I planned to sneak in later, after Bonnie was asleep and everyone had gone to bed, and check on them then.

Later that night I got a very big surprise. Bonnie had baby Linda in the bed with her, cuddling her closely. I noticed on her toy box two of my other dolls. I gasped as I noticed that both had arms that were missing. I scrambled along the floor trying to find the arms. I quietly opened the toy box and found nothing but blocks and stuffed animals in there. Upon further inspection I found the two missing arms underneath her bed and sat on the floor with tears running down my cheeks, as I tried to replace them on to Teri Lee and Linda. The nightlight was very dim, however, and I just couldn't do it.

In my opinion Bonnie wasn't old enough to play with those delicate dolls anyway and wondered why I had not been consulted. I shouldn't have been surprised because I was never asked anything but was always told. The situation that then faced me was different to others. My friends who had stood by me for so long, rested in the hands of another little girl who I knew wouldn't take care of them as I had.

It wasn't Bonnie's fault. She was just a little girl but I felt she didn't need them in the same way I did. She never had to go to Mama and Papa's house. Even though I was so upset about the dolls I was relieved Bonnie didn't have to visit on weekends. I would not want her to go through the things that I had. Sitting there that night on the floor of my sister's room, even in the midst of my loss, I was thankful that she was safe.

The thought of her having to go to my grandparents at the weekends was something I didn't want to ever have to consider. If the day ever came when she was required to go I determined to stay up all night to make sure she was safe. I would not have let my grandfather hurt her like he did me. I looked down fondly as she slept quietly holding baby Linda. She was so innocent looking and deep down inside I wasn't upset with her. At the time I just wasn't sure who was to blame. All I knew was that now I was almost completely on my own. All the things that I felt I could have counted on were slowly being ripped away from me. I felt as if my heart was torn in a million pieces just like the arms that were torn from the bodies of the two dolls. I wondered if the nightmare would ever end.

Little did I know, on the night that I sat on the floor attempting to reattach my doll's arms, that my regular weekend visits would soon come to an abrupt end, but not without grave emotional consequences. On that final weekend that I stayed at my grandparent's house, I took a bold stand with Papa, one which I had been unable to make for the previous decade. Mama was again working second shift on her job. It was at times like that where he took advantage of her absence in order to abuse me. This time I was persistent in fighting him off, something that I had not been able to do up to that point. After his initial attempt, I had just drifted off to sleep when I was awakened by the sound of gunfire. I sat up in bed startled and was afraid to move.

The next thing I remember was the light being switched on in my bedroom and my grandfather standing at the door, holding a shotgun, and telling me my grandmother was dead. Papa placed a large potato chip can on the bed beside me and gave graphic details of what it contained. I never opened the can but, believing him, sat on that bed for a grueling fifteen minutes as I cradled it in my arms. In my mind, I went again to that special 'room' which I reserved for times of severe crisis. My only reprieve was the sound of a closing car door and the realization that my grandmother was home from work safe and sound. Papa snarled, as he snatched the potato chip can from me, "The jokes on you!" By the time my grandmother turned the key in the lock I had heard the pantry door close after he had replaced the tin, and my grandfather himself had slipped into bed as if nothing had happened.

I cannot recall to this day how I convinced my mom that I should not return to my grandparent's house to spend any more nights there. But for whatever reason, the most important fact was that I never stayed another night with them, until years later when I was to move back into that house where most of the horrendous things happened. Until then I would be free from the memories of that night because I succeeded in blocking them out, but couldn't escape the effects of the serious wounds that had been inflicted upon my life.

One era had ended, but another was just beginning. My strongholds were built and my fortresses were in place. My life would now take on a new sequence of circumstances that would lead me into places I had never gone before. I was finally safe from the groping hands of the grandfather with the hideous mustache, but the effects of those fourteen years of abuse would stay with me for another forty two years.

There seemed nothing better than hands dripping with butter
and tugging on long strings of molasses candy,
as we laughed and talked about boys…

CHAPTER 14

Teenage Years

My newly gained opportunity of being able to stay home at weekends was beginning to transform my life from one of fear to one of freedom and independence. This concept was very new to me and the fact that I had, for the past ten years, spent practically every weekend in the country with my grandparents, became less prominent in my thinking. Each day the recollections became less distinct as they slowly faded into the tattered pool of memories which my mind continued to block.

I began to enjoy the weekends with some of my friends including times when we would make pizza from scratch, and other occasions when we would have 'taffy pulls' or slumber parties with some of my special girl friends. There seemed nothing better than hands dripping with butter and tugging on long strings of molasses candy, as we laughed and talked about boys. Most of us were too shy to speak to them but they still provided us with conversation points in the middle of our nights together. We wore fuzzy slippers and would sit up for hours, hair in big pink curlers, talking about everything, even the class clowns who often kept us in stitches.

I still had nightmares but most of the time couldn't remember what they had been about the next morning. That was a relief in that many nights I would wake up in a cold sweat, stifling any desire to scream out. I was trying to build more trust with my mom who for so many years had been afraid to let me leave the house. My grandparents visited often and even though my grandmother hinted that she would like for me to spend the weekend at their house, I wasn't forced to go. My incidents of self abuse were much less frequent at that time, but when they did happen I found more creative ways of concealing them.

When my grandparents were around, and they often seemed to be, it was as if a dark cloud would cover me for days following their visits. My mom, dad, sister and I would often go to their house for Sunday dinner. I always avoided going near the hall closet which use to house my beloved dolls. The three remaining ones were safely hidden in the big closet in my bedroom beneath a stack of blankets. I would still take them out on occasion and try to recapture some of the comfort they had given me when spread out on the floor of that room which I had now forsaken. I found that it wasn't the same anymore with my dolls, plus my urge to play with them now had to be hidden. Although the times that I felt they were needed were not as extreme or frequent, there were occasions when I sensed them calling to me, sometimes in whispers and sometimes louder, often with phrases of condemnation telling me what a naughty girl I had been. There had been a complete turn around and my once sincere friends and confidantes seemed to have become my foes.

I buried myself in my music for solace. My mom said she was able to detect my moods by the way I would play the piano. When I was in a happy mood I would play lively pieces but when in a solemn frame of mind she would comment about the style of music I chose to play or even how hard I was hitting the keys.

When at the piano I could lose myself in the mastery of classical pieces. My mother would often stand by me, as I sat on the piano bench, nodding out each note I played for her. She remained in her watchful position until I hit a wrong note. The first sign of faltering on my part and she would immediately walk out of the room. Even though she didn't deliberately slight me, her actions left an impression that it was necessary to be perfect in order to be accepted, and that the consequence of imperfection was abandonment. This bitter root would later require a lot of effort to remove from my 'garden of weeds'. My mental 'garden' was well overgrown by that time with every type of weed imaginable. Days came and went and I adopted the guise of living, but in reality was just coping.

There were times that I just couldn't grasp who I was or where I was going. My days of fantasy were fading and my personality was somehow being replaced by an outward shell of the little girl I use to be; a little girl with secrets she could never tell and still overshadowed by the piercing eyes of the grandfather whenever he was around or when she thought about him. The fact that I no longer spent fearful nights in the country didn't compensate for the emptiness I felt inside.

I found it hard to believe that I was finally a senior in High School. My life had actually seemed to return to normal; well the world's perception of normal, although I didn't have it firmly established in my own mind what the word normal really meant. My urge to self abuse seemed to be weaker and my times of disassociating were less frequent. Finally my grades at school were beginning to improve, according to what my guidance counselor told my mom. I was encouraged to apply myself whenever the opportunity presented itself, because there were various scholarships that would be available when it was time to go to college. I would actually be leaving home. The thought of that prospect and of not having to see my grandfather, for extended periods of time, filled me with excitement. My desire was to be a counselor so that I could help others who were in the plight of being called crazy by family and friends, which had been my experience. Maybe I would be able to encourage others who were as lonely as I had been at times. My mother wanted me to major in music, but as much as I loved it I felt psychology needed to be my goal. I could always do a minor in music.

There were still things that I didn't understand about myself even though my life was a lot simpler than it had been for so many years. I still had bouts of unexplained depression but I just wasn't able to share my feelings with anyone. Even though my friend Jean had moved to Florida when I was twelve, I still missed her a lot. There was always something so special about Jean and the friendship we shared. It was as if we were kindred spirits and, even though we never discussed personal things, I had thought many times that I would love to have shared some of my secrets with her. The last time she had seen me was when my almost lifeless body was lying at the bottom of the steps at the First Baptist Church. Even though I had not been able to share secrets I wanted to think that perhaps she somehow knew. Those hidden things were not mentioned to anyone and still remained with the dolls that I had long since set aside. The emotional upheavals were still there in spite of the fun things that my friends and I did together.

During my sophomore year I struggled through mathematics and had even failed Algebra 1, mainly because my concentration was poor. Sometimes the voices in my head would be loud but still not exceeding the sound of my grandmother's disapproval when she found out that I had a failing grade on my report card. The following year I had to repeat the same algebra class and my report card showed straight A's. The summer before I officially became a senior I had to take Geometry in summer school. While all my other friends were swimming and going on beach trips I was busy learning my formulas and taking tests. It was worth all the effort though, when I saw the A+ grade I had received which made me eligible to be a fully-fledged 'senior'.

That was absolutely my best year in school. I had been selected as a senior superlative and the title given to me was 'Most Courteous' which was quite an honor. I was also president of Christian Youth. I still didn't feel that I knew much about God but it was nice to be accepted in such a worthy organization. One of my teachers had also talked to some of us who took piano lessons to see if we could arrange to play 'Pomp and Circumstance' on Senior Day, which would be coming up a few months later. There were four of us who were taught by same piano teacher and so we mentioned to her that we had been asked to play. She selected an arrangement of the song, which turned out to be a two piano, eight handed piece.

Unfortunately my part required me to play the bass notes on one of the pianos. The technique of playing bass notes with both hands was very complicated. The rhythm was complex and, because it had to be played exactly on the beat, proved to be a challenge. That was a really tough music assignment for me and so I had to spend a lot of time preparing for the performance. I was very tempted to give up on that particular one, but mother had always said that once you began a project you shouldn't stop until it had been completed. After about a month of concentrated practice all four of us were told by Mrs. Ellis, our piano teacher, that we were skilled enough to play for the upcoming event. This gave us plenty of time to spare so that we were not rushed right before the performance.

I planned on going to my first prom in the spring with a boy named Danny. He was a wonderful dancer and even though I had taken dancing lessons when I was younger I wasn't as comfortable with the latest dance crazes. I was determined to go though, especially since I had backed out of attending the previous year, immediately before the prom. I really felt bad about letting my date down and this time I wanted to be accepted by my group of peers. Dating wasn't something that I particularly felt at ease with although I had gone on a few dates. I didn't take long to adjust to it, particularly following some gentle persuasion from my friends telling me that all seniors dated.

During my junior year I had dated Aunt Ruth's pastor's son. She had arranged that we would both attend the same church hayride. It was on this hayride that he had held my hand and sang the song, 'Roses Are Red.' He was very handsome and I found out very quickly that there was a lot of competition to gain his attention. I decided that it wasn't worth the effort and so we didn't date for very long.

I felt that I had fallen in love with Danny, my high school prom date, although my mom didn't share my enthusiasm. Her main concern was that he didn't attend church and so may not have a positive influence on me. I was constantly told that any date could be a potential husband and therefore he wasn't a good choice. She did allow me, however, to go to the prom with him and reluctantly let me double date with a friend of mine named Donna and her boyfriend. I wasn't allowed to single date very much at all during high school.

If my mom had known how afraid I was of boys she wouldn't have had the concerns that she did, especially ones where I might be intimate with any of them. I stood firm on my conviction of not being 'loose' as some of the girls were in our class. All the girls who were virgins wore 'virgin pins' which was really a sterling silver ring that was worn on the collar. If a girl didn't wear one of these pins she

was an easy target for anyone who wanted more than just a friendship. Every single time I put this pin on there was a gnawing feeling
of guilt and shame that welled up inside of me. It was on occasions
such as this that I would think of my white handkerchief, which had
been safely hidden in its secret compartment in my closet. By then
it was concealed in a different closet and not the one at the house
where we had lived a few blocks from town.

When I was in the seventh grade we moved into a new home,
this time a beautiful one, newly constructed, with bright, shiny hard-
wood floors. I felt like a princess in our new home and it was so
different from the first house I had remembered living in, with the
one bedroom. My dad was then financially able to buy us a new house
and I remember the excitement of having a big bedroom in a house
that no one else had lived in before. It seemed so many years ago that
we had lived on Mrs. Fuller's land. There were a lot of good memories in the small house with those tiny three rooms, one being my safe
Friday nights with my mom. Another was my afternoon excursion
when I had praised and really talked to God for the first time, and also
my friendship with Donald, the boy who so exasperated me.

The day finally came that spring of 1964 when three of my classmates and I played 'Pomp and Circumstance' on two pianos that had
been rented for the class day. We took our places at the piano and
as we performed the very long rendition of this song I played with
total confidence and don't recall missing a note. I had total clarity
of mind and all of the hard work and theory that I had learned at the
hands of my very strict teacher had paid off. We received a standing
ovation from the students who crowded the gym. I was reminded of
the story my mom had written of Abram Dabosky and as the audience applauded I could almost hear a voice saying, "Well done." It
was times like that when I could again feel the presence of the God
that I still knew very little about. I felt that He certainly was in the
gym that morning in May; just like He had been in the pasture that
summer afternoon and on the night I received my crown in Girl's
Auxiliary. I knew that this God, who had visited me, on more than
one occasion, was real and He was calling out my name. It may have
seemed silly to some, but to me it was real. I wasn't sure at this time
how to keep His presence with me always.

I had figured out a way to keep the dolls with me so that I could still experience their comfort in my life. The question was how I could keep God with me as well. I wasn't sure how that one would be resolved or even if it could be, but as my mom had repeated so many times, "Don't give up on a project you have started." I wondered if I had started a project trying to find God. I had only encountered Him on the three occasions. I didn't feel it was a project exactly, but more like a wish to have those feelings of peace that had been with me at those times I knew He was around. It was a mystery but just maybe something I might need to pursue.

I just wanted to get out of town and away from all the unhappy memories, hoping that maybe new surroundings would give me a better perspective on life…

CHAPTER 15

The Runaway

Graduation came and went quickly and I was now a high school graduate and had been accepted at North Greenville Junior College. It was a happy occasion mixed with tinges of sadness, as my friends and I would be going our separate ways. I did have one classmate, Joan, who would also be attending North Greenville and it comforted me knowing that there was at least one person that I would know going there. Although I was excited about this next chapter of my life my biggest apprehension was that I would be leaving Danny.

My mom couldn't be any happier because she was praying that my time away would get my mind off the young man, who I had become so attached to during my last two years in high school. She continued to stand firm in the fact that he wasn't right for me and had basically forbidden me to date him. That didn't seem to work because I usually found a way to slip out and see him some Saturday nights with the help of a few of my friends. To me lying wasn't such a bad thing as I had convinced myself that it was a way to keep my parents from being upset, so in my warped thinking it was acceptable.

Mother insisted on me getting a job to earn extra money which could be used to purchase things that I needed for college. I was not happy about the fact that my grandmother would be paying for my tuition. I felt that this would keep me tied to her and knew from bitter experience that any contribution from Mama usually had strings attached to it. I had long since tried to sever former ties although most of my attempts failed.

I was encouraged to save my money for the upcoming college days but didn't actually earn very much at McClellan's Dime Store. I probably spent half my pay check on goodies for me and my friends since I worked in the candy department at the store. My work experience was more of an attempt by my mom to keep me occupied and away from Danny than it was to raise funds for college. In that respect it succeeded.

One thing that bothered me about the place where I worked was the fact that there at the back of the store were two water fountains. One was clearly marked 'White' and the other labeled 'Colored'. This racial bigotry had always been a pet peeve of mine, like having separate waiting rooms at the doctor's office where I spent so much time while growing up. This issue of skin color did not in any way make sense to me, nor why the majority of the people that I knew felt the way that they did, especially my grandparents and uncles.

During the summer break, before going to college, some of my friends and I drove to Greenwood on the Saturday nights so that we could cruise around the 'Ranch' a local restaurant, although our favorite place was the 'Kum Back' which was located in Abbeville. 'Cruising' was a favorite pastime at weekends. It was amazing how much enjoyment we found in driving past the same restaurant time and time again, often just to wave at friends we knew. It was also a means by which we could gather and figure out how we were going to get past the next restriction our parents were going to set. We felt we had a pretty good thing going for the most part. Whoever had permission to use the family car was the one privileged to drive us all around. With our parents feeling there was safety in numbers we didn't usually have a problem finding a vehicle or a driver.

This is really the time that Susan and I didn't do as much together as we once had. Since her father was the minister at the church, she had stricter curfews imposed on her than we did. I still stayed in close contact with her concerning my boyfriend Danny, and asked for any advice on how I could possibly convince my mom that he was really a fine young man. I hated the pressure that was being put on me concerning Danny and also the pressure of the upcoming September at North Greenville Junior College. I had never felt I could meet up to anyone's expectations and this was no exception.

Nothing seemed to work and I for some hair brained reason felt that maybe a change of scenery might make my mom appreciate me more. I wasn't sure what had been going on in my mind since I graduated but it all smelled like freedom and the thoughts of again having someone run my life wasn't what I wanted. As selfish and self centered as that sounds, it was how I felt at the time so I went on my impulses and planned to buy a one way ticket to Bowie Maryland, to stay with a cousin there. The only problem was that I didn't have the $14.28 that was necessary for the ticket. There had to be a way to get the money. The brainstorm I had was nothing less than genius. My mother was Sunday School Treasurer and so I would borrow the money from her. Then I would take a month off, work for my cousin in Maryland, come back and return the money, hopefully before it was even missed. My reasoning was that things would look a whole lot better on my return and then perhaps my mother would realize just how serious I was about Danny.

All my plans were made and I only told one friend and that was Susan. Now even though Susan was my true friend, she wasn't going to let me leave town with a one way ticket without telling someone. My mom and dad were out of town at that time for some type of church meeting and I was staying at Susan's house. We discussed the whole plan the night before and she tried to talk me out of running away. I explained to her it wasn't that I wouldn't ever come back but right then I just needed time to think. I was relieved that I no longer had to stay with Mama and Papa while my parent's were gone. Susan spent half the night trying to talk me out of my ridiculous plan but she didn't succeed. So that next night, at approximately 8:15 pm, a couple of my friends picked me up at Susan's house while her parent's were at a church staff meeting. I hugged her and she sadly watched me leave.

Just as I arrived at the train station and got my ticket I saw my grandmother's car drive up nearby. She bolted out of the car and tried to reason with me. I told her that I was leaving and that she couldn't stop me but did say that I would call after I got to my destination. I knew then that Susan had revealed my plans but then I probably would have done the same thing had I been in her place. I wasn't mad at Susan. I just wanted to get out of town and away from all the unhappy memories, hoping that maybe new surroundings would give me a better perspective on life.

As I handed my baggage to the conductor and made my way to a seat, I could see my grandmother's car still parked outside the station. I imagined she was sitting there solemnly considering her inability to maintain her hold on me, as the train began to roll down the tracks carrying her granddaughter with a one way ticket to Bowie, Maryland. In my mind I was ditching that town and going to the big city. It could be that going to college just wasn't what I wanted after all. I knew I wanted Danny but that seemed impossible.

I had many mixed feelings as I looked back to still see my grandmother's car parked in the same place. I wondered how long she would stay there. At least she hadn't brought my grandfather with her. I did feel sorry for her because I didn't want her to be worried about me. I was going to be fine. I could see myself becoming tough in a lot of ways; at least there was a part of me that seemed to be so. I wasn't quite sure I understood it right then, but because I had always been shy I found it difficult to actually picture myself on a train with a one way ticket to another city. Right then I didn't want to think of anything else except maybe a new life or some answers for the one that I already had.

I slept very little on the train journey to Bowie. There were a few frightening thoughts that troubled me as we passed through the winding farmland, and with each flicker of light from a town or train station, there was a feeling of loneliness that I hadn't been expecting. This bid for independence was something I really wanted or at least it certainly seemed that way. My parents didn't understand and perhaps they never would, and the only way that I could know what I wanted in life was to set out and find it. Mom and dad would be very upset when they found out that I had left home, as there would have been no way that they would have either given me the money or the permission to go to my cousin Marty's house, even though they loved Marty.

She was the daughter of Uncle Furman, my grandmother's brother, and she and her husband Joe lived in Bowie not very far from Washington D.C. They had one young son, Anthony. My family and I had visited them on several occasions. Once when I was fourteen, our visit to them had been unpleasant for me because of the presence of my grandfather, but I immediately felt safe with Marty and Joe. I had wished then that I didn't have to go back home and had fantasies of living with them. Marty was a Christian and she had a wonderful personality, very similar to that of Marjorie Sanders. It was no big surprise to me that I would now, at this point in my life, again try to find a safe place.

I had made no formal announcement about my upcoming visit to their house, but just acted on impulse. "How foolish I had been!" I reprimanded myself, as I thought of the possibility of them not even being home. I knew that Barry, my cousin, was in Washington at the time because he was working as a Page in Congressman Dorn's office. I knew that he could be contacted even if Marty and Joe were not at home. At any rate the important thing was that I finally had the nerve to leave Abbeville, the place where the horrors had all begun. I was hoping that this would be the time to make some sense out of my life, what I could remember of it.

At this point I was emotionally unstable and not in a position to make rational decisions. No time during the long train ride did I give thought to the consequences of my actions or how it could affect anyone else. Through this and other actions I could see myself turning into a very self centered young lady at seventeen. I didn't want anyone controlling my life and most of all I hated the fact that my mom refused to let me date Danny. Perhaps my time away would give her something to think about and would let her know how serious I was about becoming an adult. The thought had also crossed my mind that I had already been forced to be an 'adult' for a long time against my will, and much earlier than any child should be. For this reason it should follow that I would be granted some of the privileges of an adult also.

I wondered how God viewed me, although I hadn't seen many instances where I felt He had helped me out of difficult situations. I justified my criminal act by assuring myself that I would pay back the money I had taken from my mom at some point in time, thus canceling out the seriousness of what I had done. My head began to pound. I hadn't thought of bringing a sandwich and I only had a little money left for emergencies. I did remember to put an apple in my bag so at about four in the morning I decided it was time for a snack. Maybe that would help my headache. Resting my head against the back of the seat, I thought again of what a horrible sinner I was, not just a runaway but also a thief. I wondered if there was some way to regain the innocence felt that afternoon in the pasture behind our first house, or was I doomed to be that young girl always running and hiding, as she had done so many times on Saturday nights at her grandparent's house.

I drifted off to sleep amidst the questions, fears, and uncertainties of that summer night in 1964. I awoke to the conductor telling me that I had reached my destination. I wearily gathered up my bag and went to the checkout to wait for my other luggage. For about an hour I sat on the wooden seats outside the train station before eventually mustering the courage to call Marty to tell her that I was in town. I admitted that I had run away from home. She commented that we would discuss it when she came to pick me up. I asked her to wait before calling my mom until we had a chance to talk. Marty agreed and I felt quite a sense of relief when she arrived at the train station.

She said Joe was at work and would be happy to see me also. Anthony was about three years old and this was the first time that I had seen him. Marty and Joe had adopted Anthony when he was about a year old. I had seen a picture of him once but it was exciting to finally see him in person. It made me a bit sad to think about my own sister who was now seven and wondered if she would miss me as much as I would her. For the first time in my life I had begun to get close to Bonnie and then just as we were beginning to bond, I chose to run away from home.

Life seemed to be so complicated and I had wondered if Marty would be able to help me sort out this entire problem, because I had not done too well on my own. I was so unsure by then of my college plans and my future with Danny and had no desire to meet up with my grandfather again. I could still picture my grandmother sitting in her car as the train left the station and that made me feel sad for her.

Anyone leaving, whether it was me or someone else, seemed to be a trigger to the overwhelming feeling of abandonment within me.

My cousin's house was just as I had remembered it at fourteen. Joe was friendly as always and seemed to be very glad to see me. It was well into the afternoon before I really had a chance to talk with Marty about why I had left home. She persuaded me to call my grandmother to let her know that I was with them and therefore safe. I would have to wait on the consequences of what my parents would say once they found out that I was in Maryland. I was almost sure by now that someone had contacted them and wasn't at all anxious to talk to my mom.

For a moment I felt as if I had died and gone to heaven. Here I was about fourteen hours from home; no grandfather in sight and staying with one of my favorite cousins and having the bonus of Barry, my other favorite cousin, only about twenty miles away. Marty had called him before dinner to let him know that I was there and asked him to come over one night soon.. He seemed to be in a big hurry when she phoned him and said he would see what he could work out and then get back to us. He was very inquisitive about how I happened to end up in Maryland but Marty just told him she would explain when he came over. She laughed as she hung up the phone. "That is one sure way of getting him over here," she teased, knowing full well he would want to know all the juicy gossip. I swore her to secrecy about anything concerning Danny. I knew that I was in enough trouble with my mom without her thinking that Danny could have had anything to do with my decision to leave home.

We had a pleasant dinner that night with Anthony entertaining us as he sent peas flying Joe's way. Joe giggled and gave him a playful pinch on the cheek. "This is great," I thought to myself. It was hard to remember a time where I felt so free and safe as that, except for those Friday nights many years ago on Mrs. Fuller's property, enjoying the company of my mom. Marty and Joe were really down to earth and what made it so special to be with them was that they weren't condemning. Even when I told Marty that I had run away from home she didn't put me down or make me feel bad about myself. Instead she reassured me that we would work it all out and I just needed to take one day at a time.

After dinner I offered to help Marty with the dishes, in much the same way I use to help my mom. We talked more about my problems with Danny and my mother's insistence that I shouldn't date him. Marty pointed out that she was convinced that God gave mothers an extra sense, one that enabled them to scout out danger much like a mother lion would do with her cubs to keep them from harm. I hated it when adults made sense! I just listened politely, but wasn't going to verbally agree with anything, especially when it came to Danny, the young man whom I loved.

Marty said that Mama had called before dinner to say that my family would be returning home the next day, so I would need to talk to my mom on the phone. This confrontation wasn't going to be easy but then neither was my decision to leave home and come to Maryland in the first place. Surely I would be able to handle one mom, on the other end of the phone, a mere fourteen hours train journey away, wouldn't I? It was time to implement some very well thought out strategy. Suddenly the idea of being an adult began to lose its glamour. I didn't sleep very well that night as I contemplated how I would explain my actions of the past few days.

This wasn't my fantasy world now. It was real and the decisions that I was making were ultimately going to affect my life...

CHAPTER 16

The Prodigal Returns

There was no way to avoid the inevitable conflict that came with explaining to my mom how I had found myself in the State of Maryland while she, my dad and sister had gone to Myrtle, Mississippi for a church camp meeting. I think just hearing the disappointment in her voice affected me more than anything else and the fact that I again had not behaved responsibly. She was emphatic in her questioning of my motives and wondered what I could possibly have been thinking of at the time. I really had no answer for her except that this was done on an impulse. She asked me how I intended to get back home and I had to try to explain to her that returning home wasn't an option to be considered. Instead I wanted to stay in Maryland, find a job and attend the university there. Returning to Abbeville just wasn't in my agenda for the immediate future.

My mom seemed to always know what I was thinking, especially when it came to Danny. She immediately asked if the problems with my boyfriend had any bearing on my decision to leave. I wasn't going to lie to her and add to my list of sins, so I was honest and admitted I was very upset that she wouldn't allow me to date Danny. Mother said that she was not changing her mind and that as long as I lived under her roof I would follow her guidelines. I knew that she meant it and discussing this issue wasn't going to get me anywhere.

Mother told me that I needed to think long and hard about my decision and reminded me of the fact that I was not yet eighteen years old and wouldn't be until July. She pointed out that legally she could force me to come home but instead was going to let me make my own decision, while praying that I would make the right one. My mom wasn't one to back down when she had deep convictions and had proved that many times. I did tell her I would think about what she had said. At the time I just couldn't break the news to her that I had taken money from her Sunday School Class Treasury Account. The more I thought about it the more guilty I felt. I wasn't really so much stealing from my mom as I was from God and had no confidence that He could forgive me for that particular sin. I was sure that I was doomed to hell. I had to think of some way to earn the money to pay that back. Perhaps I could do that while at Marty's house and send it to Mother. Right then I felt I needed to avoid confessing this horrendous sin to her, especially until I found a way to repay what I had stolen.

I knew that they only had Sunday School meetings every three months and that there had been one shortly before I left, so hoped that would 'buy me a little time'. I didn't tell Marty that I had stolen the money either. I knew that she was very open-minded but wouldn't approve of me stealing from God. This bothered me day and night, in a similar way to an occasion when I was five years old and had stolen a piece of gum from my neighbor. At that time I had gone next door and while at her house had asked if I could use her bathroom. There on the cabinet was a packet of gum and I carefully took one of the sticks from it. Outside, where Miss Higginbotham was washing her car, I would stop chewing every time she looked at me, as I feared she would know that the gum had come from her bathroom. Even then I must have been experiencing a feeling of guilt.

I could see where God was showing me the difference between right and wrong but obviously wasn't paying a lot of attention. I just wondered why I didn't always make the right decisions. It would be twenty years later that I would confess to that lady that I had stolen the gum. After accepting Christ I had felt it necessary to make things right with those whom I had previously offended, even if they knew nothing about the particular sin which had been committed.

At this time even though I wasn't saved, my conscience did bother me about what I had done, to the extent that I knew that I had to somehow pay that money back. Right then my priority was to find a way to make some extra cash. Maybe Barry would have a suggestion when he came to visit Marty and Joe in a few days. We were also expecting Uncle Furman to come by. Marty and I often referred to him as Uncle Furman with a 'sermon'. She had a unique sense of humor and so did I and that was one of the reasons we got along so well. I knew that I would never confess my evil deed to Uncle Furman anymore than I would to Marty. After all he was a preacher and therefore had a pre-conceived idea about sin. I felt such a rotten sinner at the time, very like the ones the preacher spoke about at the church where I use to attend. I was also an emotional cripple without the tools to climb out of the mess I had created. Right then I was going to have to carry the burden alone in much the same way as I had to carry so many 'secrets' from the past.

Uncle Furman was a teacher in Washington, D.C. His wife taught in Virginia and even though their schools kept them in different towns they would get together some weekends. It didn't seem like an ideal situation to me for a husband to be separated from his wife for long periods, but then I wasn't really sure what a real family was supposed to be like anyway. I knew mine had been far from normal and if that arrangement worked for Uncle Furman and Aunt Ruth, who was I to question it?

By coincidence there were two aunts called Ruth in our family. Both were married to my grandmother's brothers, one to Uncle Bombie and the other to her youngest brother, Uncle Furman. I sat on the bed in the guest room at Marty's house and thought a lot about the structure of a family and even at seventeen was unable to figure out how one could possibly be as confusing as mine. Through marriage Aunt Ruth, Bombie's wife, was related on both sides of the family. We often teased my mom and told her that she could possibly have married her cousin which she didn't find funny at all.

As I sat contemplating family trees and the fact that I didn't think I wanted to delve back any further to see where our roots were, there was a knock at the door. It was my Uncle Furman and I was truly hoping this time he had not come with a sermon. I had enough sermons on my mind for one day and a lot of confusing thoughts about the impossibility of figuring out our family tree. I considered my afternoon a complete waste of time and energy as how could family trees and genealogies possibly help me to sort out the problems that I had. With that lingering thought I made my way to the den to greet Uncle Furman.

He was delighted to see me and gave me a big hug and kiss on the cheek. There was never a time that Uncle Furman minced words and this occasion was no different. He came right to the point and tried to find out why I was in Maryland rather than getting ready to pack for college. I explained to him that I needed to take a break and had decided to visit Marty. He looked at me quizzically and I detected that he was reading a lot more into my explanation than I was giving. Uncle Furman began to point out that rather than say we hated something, it would be better to say we had not learned to appreciate it yet, not that it had a lot to do with what we were discussing at the time. Marty and I looked at each other with a knowing grin on our faces realizing that this must be the 'sermon' of the day. It never failed to materialize and we both enjoyed our little private joke of 'Furman with a sermon'.

I was very excited about Barry's upcoming visit and anxious to talk to him about my plans. We had always been close and how ironic it was that I had ended up in a city near him. In a conversation on the phone he told me to get ready because we would be bursting into the political party arena this coming weekend and I needed to have my impressive dress and shoes ready. He said all the Pages did was to party on weekends and that he didn't want me to miss the excitement. I told him that I would probably not mention it to Marty and Joe as they may not approve. He laughed and agreed with me. "What they don't know won't hurt them and besides haven't I always looked after you?" he eagerly prompted facetiously.

I had to chuckle at that remark and was reminded of other occasions he had done just that. Once I had been pushed into a ditch on a make-shift chariot which had been constructed out of a barrel. Another time involved the wearing of a lovely evening gown made of yellow chiffon, which proved too much for a conservative spring piano recital. It would have been appropriate had it not been for the tiny spaghetti straps and the endless supply of flowers made out of yellow tissue paper pinned to practically every inch of the dress. My only hope would be that no one would light a cigarette during the evening or I might have gone up in flames. Even though the intricate design Barry had created for me was done because of his deep love for me, my teacher pointed out the dress was just not suitable for our spring recital. I wasn't sure if I was more devastated than Barry about the gown. He was also a bit upset that I had bragged to others that my male cousin had made it for me. Unfortunately he suffered some teasing because of his handiwork and vowed that day to never make anything else in the line of clothes for me. For my part I was just so honored that he would go to such extremes on my behalf.

The more I began to hear about Washington and the fact that Barry had some close friends in high places, the more excited I became. This sounded too good to be true but I definitely wasn't going to let any of this escape me, not while I was far enough away from the critical voices of my mom, dad, and grandparents. This was to be my time for however long it would last.

After all that had happened in previous years I felt I deserved it. I would need to discuss with Marty the possibility of getting something more suitable to wear to one of the parties if the dress I had wasn't appropriate. I really wanted to go out 'on the town' and somehow I was hoping that Barry and his debonair personality would be enough to convince Marty and Joe that I would be safe with him. After all Barry worked for the government and what better credentials could he have than that!

Saturday finally came, and with it the social event of the season which I had waited all week for. In my eyes this could be like my coming out party, a debutante affair, and it might just compensate for some of the unhappiness I had been forced to be a part of in the past. Little did I know that it would take much more than an elaborate party to change my views about myself. Barry had, in his most persuasive tone, convinced Marty and Joe that I deserved a night out as that might be the last time that I would have the opportunity to see Washington. He had volunteered to be my escort and said that he would assume all personal responsibility for me and ensure that I arrived home at a respectable time. We didn't discuss curfews but Barry made it plain that I would be in good hands and that they could absolutely trust him. I found him to be pretty convincing and was hoping nothing would spoil the moment.

I had brought one dress with me that one of my friends had loaned me awhile back. I was fortunate to have some friends who were willing to exchange outfits and kept thinking this one just might be suitable for the occasion. I knew Barry would be honest with me about how it looked as he usually had good taste. Besides the prom, this would be the second most important event that I had ever attended and this time it was in Washington, D.C. There had to be some way to make me feel important. For some this may have been just a party but for me it was a way of making a statement like, "Here I am and I am somebody. I am not just a girl who was born for sex but there is more to me than that. I am worth the 'God of the Pasture' passing by and even staying with me for awhile. That white handkerchief, concealed in a secret compartment symbolizes my reluctance to be a part of the ugliness that was forced on me." I realized that maybe one day the truth would come out. It wasn't likely, but until it did I would like to still live in my fantasy world where my dreams would remain unspoiled.

It didn't take me long to discover that being 'out on the town' in Washington, D.C. was quite different from cruising the Ranch or Kum Back at home. Barry and I made our rounds on the party scene that summer night and, as exciting as it was, I realized immediately that even though I may have been way out of my league I wasn't going to let anyone know. I did find out that drinking and trying to stand up at the same time wasn't an easy task, especially for one who was only used to sharing one bottle of vodka and orange juice, something we did rarely and referred to as 'Passing The Tommy'.

I was seventeen but I am sure that I drank as much as any eighteen year old might on their first binge. It wasn't clear if Barry was holding me up or if I was holding him up by the end of the evening. I liked the excitement of meeting new people, but this was 'big time' for me and took my social awareness to new heights. By the time we ended up at a coffee shop to help us sober up before the trip back to Marty and Joe's house, my head was spinning. I had to make several trips to the bathroom and any thought of breakfast food at this time was most unappealing. I managed to get through two cups of black coffee and on the ride back home all I could think about was the questions I might be asked about my night out.

It was past midnight and I soon realized that the 'Potters' had already gone to bed. I suggested to Barry that he should stay the night as I wasn't sure he was in any condition to continue driving. He assured me he would be fine and would give me a call the following afternoon. As I heard him drive off, I quickly went to the bathroom to wash my face and get ready for bed because I was so exhausted. In spite of my tiredness sleep just wouldn't come that night. There were so many things on my mind. I was thinking about the future, about the decisions I had made and the major question of how I had ended up in Maryland when I was supposed to be at home, making plans to go to college.

This wasn't my fantasy world now. It was real and the decisions that I was making were ultimately going to affect my life. I had no money to support myself and if I stayed with Marty and Joe I was going to have to get a job. My tuition to the university in Maryland would not be paid for me like it would be at home. I had made no plans and could not think of one positive action I had taken since finishing high school. There was also the issue of the money I had stolen from my mom, which I knew had to be paid back. My mind questioned whether things would ever return to normal. I realized by then that the trip to Washington hadn't been a good idea.

And then there was Danny. I couldn't even talk to him on the phone. I wondered if he missed me as much as I missed him. I also had to face up to the fact that even if I did go back home, dating him was out of the question. I didn't like being deceitful and I had secretly slipped out to meet him on more than one occasion and always wondered how my mom knew. She kept reminding me of her God-given ability to know a lot more than I gave her credit for.

It was almost five in the morning before I finally drifted off to sleep. I was awakened by Marty opening the drapes and saying, "Good morning, merry sunshine, breakfast time." I wanted to throw my pillow at her. I hadn't made a formal announcement that I was not a morning person and didn't feel this would be an appropriate way to do it, so I refrained from anything except, a half whispered, "Morning, Marty." She was always in a good mood and probably the most positive person in our family. I guess that was one of the things that had drawn me to her and the fact that I did feel safe in her company.

In spite of the fact that this was a safe place to be, it didn't take me more than a few days to make yet another decision, and that was to return home. Barry would be driving back to Abbeville in less than a week because his internship was over at Bryan Dorn's office. I would be able to ride back with him. Even though running away at the time had seemed the right thing to do, I knew by then that it wasn't, and I needed to go back home and face those things, or least some of the ones I had been running away from. Marty was disappointed that I wouldn't be staying longer but I knew this wasn't the way to start a new life and maybe going back home would somehow restore me into my mom's good graces, or at least that was my hope.

*Daddy talked about godly repentance and although
I had heard the term before, at that time the true meaning of what
he said escaped me...*

CHAPTER 17

Tough Love

In less than a week, Barry and I said our goodbyes and began making our way back to Abbeville from Marty and Joe's house. It was about a fourteen hour trip and because Barry was driving a government car we seemed to break every speeding law from Maryland to South Carolina, taking advantage of a privileged license plate which contained only one number and letter. Barry found it amusing to watch me clinging to the hand rail as I pleaded with him to slow down. It was good to be with him though and we talked about a lot of things on the journey although I made sure my negative past wasn't one of them. We had quite a few laughs reminiscing about our escapades as we were growing up and I reminded him how I had forever cured him of biting me by retaliating at the age of three.

It was good to have the long miles ahead of us so that I could postpone thinking of the issues to be faced on my arrival home. The fact was, I almost felt like a criminal being extradited to the state where the crime had taken place, each time I thought of the money that had been taken from my mom's chest of drawers. In retrospect it seemed like a cold, callous act which had been committed and one which could never warrant forgiveness, and in my mom's eyes would be adding to my growing list of betrayals.

I thought about the thief on the cross and wondered what his pillage had been. God came into my mind also in spite of the fact that I really wasn't so sure how much He was actually thinking about me. I fantasized many times about the event in the pasture, and of the few occasions that I had actually sensed His presence. I knew God was real and I did believe in Him. I had even admitted as much to the preacher when I shook his hand at twelve years old. I was keenly aware there was something missing in my life, but those times when I really tried to concentrate on a more personal God would be interrupted by the word 'sinner' ringing through my ears as if amplified from some external judge. I thought about introducing the subject of God as I talked with Barry but I just couldn't bring myself to do it.

Even though I got along well with Barry, there were things which I didn't share with him. For example I had not gathered the courage to tell him much about my relationship with Danny or my mother's disapproval of him. It wasn't something you usually talked about with a person of the opposite sex. Even though Barry fished around for answers to explain my impulsive train ride to Maryland, he soon sensed my reluctance to discuss it and dropped the subject.

Barry was the closest thing I had to an older brother. He was wise beyond his years, had great aspirations of becoming an interior designer and had even picked out the school he would attend in New York. His artwork was impressive and some select pieces had found a home in his mother's living room. Aunt Grace would invite all of her friends over to see the mural he had painted on the wall, and admire the real waterfall cascading over greenery set in various places around the room. It was almost like walking into a rain forest although very tastefully done. He had also included sound effects of various live birds in cages which added to the atmosphere.

It is amazing what thoughts come to mind when trying to escape unpleasant memories. Barry's artistic theme of the forest made me think both of my love of trees and my hate of them at the same time. I struggled to keep my thoughts focused on the beauty of the mural instead of the creepy frightening branches of trees that could have possibly held me captive. For a moment I began to hear the voices in my head again even more prominently than the music that Barry was playing on the car radio. It had been months since I had been troubled by such thoughts and they then hit me with renewed vigor giving me the feeling that my breath had been completely expelled from my lungs.

Once the thought process had been set in motion many flashbacks began to flood in. I began to think of weekends in the country, the barn, the potato chip can, and the gunshot. These probably only lasted for a few seconds although it seemed a lot longer. The next thing I remember was Barry pulling into a gas station. We were within a few hours of home. That was not a refreshing thought although getting through the inquisition would be only a one-time event; at least I hoped that would be the case.

There are many times in life when it seems difficult to find words to express what you want to say. I, at seventeen years old, had experienced moments like that and this recent one would be no exception. Barry and I had agreed ahead of time that it would be best if he didn't come inside once we were home. I didn't want him to be involved in any unpleasant 'fireworks display' upon my arrival. He carefully lifted my baggage out of his trunk and left it in the carport, gave me a swift hug and a kiss on the forehead and wished me good luck. I gave him a somewhat puppy-dog look as he made his escape in the car. He glanced back at me with a thumb up sign which gave me a bit more courage, as I gathered what was left of my very weakened composure to walk into that den where my mom and dad were.

I just stood there for a moment after going inside. My mom was cooking and my dad was sitting in his favorite chair. He didn't get up but smiled at me as if nothing had happened. "Welcome home sis." This had become my nickname since Bonnie was born. Daddy had his Bible sitting on his lap, which wasn't at all unusual as he studied constantly, that is if he wasn't out fishing. He was not the disciplinarian of the family, however, so I knew that getting past him wasn't going to be the problem. Mother continued to cook and suggested that I get my luggage unpacked and that we would talk after we had dinner. Eating was the last thing on my mind but I quickly obeyed and went to retrieve the rest of my things from the carport, carrying them directly into my room.

Once my belongings were back in place I asked my mom if she needed any help with the dinner and also tried to find out where my sister was. Mother said she was with Aunt Ruth and Bombie and they would be bringing her home later. I was convinced my parents didn't want Bonnie at the house when we had our talk. No help with the dinner was needed so Mother suggested I go take a bath. I had the urge to call Danny but knew that I would not be able to get past my mom's scrutiny. It was evident that I would be watched for quite awhile or at least until it was time to leave for college.

Mother called from the kitchen as I was about to take my shower and suggested that it would be polite of me to call Mama and let her know that I had arrived home safely. As a virtual prisoner my solitary phone call was obviously going to be to my grandparent's house. I was really hoping my grandfather wouldn't answer. As luck would have it, Mama did answer the phone and she was glad to hear from me, managing to hold back anything negative that I had been anticipating from her.

There wasn't a lot of conversation during dinner. Daddy talked about his last fishing trip and cracked a few jokes as usual. I sensed he was trying to make me feel a bit more at ease but it didn't work. My mom hadn't yet shown any type of emotion, but in spite of that, I could visualize myself in front of a firing squad, hood over my head, hands behind my back and waiting for the inevitable moment when I would feel the sting of the bullet strike me. In comparison I knew no bullet could possibly make me feel as wounded as the effects of what my mom might say. She was not a woman who exhibited anger but what I detected was extreme disappointment and that hurt far more than any executioner's bullet. It was an immense struggle to swallow and I could feel the food getting lodged about half way down my throat. I was trapped, a fugitive now home, awaiting the inquisition that would inevitably follow.

The situation was serious. The worst part about it was that I knew how wrong it was to disobey my parents and to steal. It wasn't that I had not been taught that these things were a sin for I had heard about the Ten Commandments as long as I could remember and for some reason the command to not steal was the one that stood out most to me. The reason for this might have been that I felt so much had been taken from me while growing up, being deprived of weekends with my parents making up the biggest factor. I found myself questioning why I was again focusing on my past abuse rather than my sin. It was true. I was a horrible sinner. The present issue wasn't about me. It was about the fact that I had made some very wrong choices and so needed to face up to what I had done.

Mother was the first to speak. She looked at me, void of any anger, and yet it was difficult to look her directly in the eyes. "Claudette, I already knew that money was missing from my Sunday school account and it was obvious to me that you were the one who took it." "I don't know what possessed you to do what you did and I can't accept any excuses for your action, but tonight there are some things we are going to get straight." She continued firmly, "First of all you will pay back the money you stole and I am multiplying the amount owed, three times, which means it will take you quite awhile to earn it. If your job is no longer available at McClellan's then you will need to find another one until it is time to attend North Greenville."

Then she became even sterner and emphasized, "There will be no more dates with Danny. If you disobey us and go out with him, your bags will be packed and placed in the carport when you return." Her argument gained strength as she continued with confidence and authority, "Your father and I have discussed this and are adamant that you will not live in this house if you continue to defy us. The rebellion is over." Her voice softened a little as she said, "I love you and your daddy loves you too but God has made us responsible for your wellbeing and that means that for the moment we make the decisions. If you have something you want to say, a comment or a question maybe, now is the time to do it. We want to be sure you understand the rules." With that she sat back in her chair to await my response.

I did understand her ultimatum very well and for the first time I knew, beyond a shadow of a doubt that Mother was serious and she would do exactly as she had threatened if I didn't come into line with the guidelines she and daddy laid down. By the end of her lecture I was crying uncontrollably. She told me that there was a lot that needed to be done on my part in order to rebuild the trust that had been broken. Daddy talked about godly repentance and although I had heard the term before, at that time the true meaning of what he said escaped me. Many years would pass before I would get the full impact of that statement. For the time being the crisis was over and for me a new life could be beginning, or so I was assured if I was serious about my future. I determined that at least I was going to give it a try. My mom had established a firm stance with me the day I returned home from Maryland, one that would be brought to my attention many times in the years to come. I had learned the meaning of 'tough love'.

All that I was interested in was, that in a matter of months I would be relocating to a 'woodsy area' called Tigerville, South Carolina and leaving Abbeville behind …

CHAPTER 18

College Days

The incident of the theft of the money, so ruthlessly taken from the Sunday school account, began to fade in my memory as weekly repayments were made to my mom. Danny was out of the picture physically, as I had made a sincere promise to my parents that I would under no circumstances date him again. The 'prodigal' daughter had returned home from Maryland, not because she felt an overwhelming urge to get out of a 'pig pen' mode of life, so eloquently spoken of in the Bible, but because of the knowledge that this was the next phase of life. If there was something of worth around the bend then Sarah Claudette Hammond Cooper had to find it. Ideally speaking, conviction and right moral standing should have been the motive, but with such a lack of maturity and a wide variety of dysfunctional upbringing, this was all that surfaced in the summer of sixty four.

I felt I had a real edge over most of the future college kids, being privy to information that they wouldn't have. I was the only potential North Greenville graduate from Abbeville who would know a lot about her roommate in advance. An article had appeared in one of the local newspapers about a young lady named Sheila Hilley, a resident of Broadway Lake in Anderson, South Carolina. The amazing fact to me was, that she would be my roommate at North Greenville. I sat on my bed with great excitement and read the story of the blind girl from Anderson, who could do many incredible things and had surmounted difficulties in spite of tragically losing her sight as a result of running in front of a car when six years old.

According to the newspaper article she had been blinded because of the horrific damage done by the car door handle as she was struck. Left for dead in a hospital morgue, an observant orderly saw her foot move and the doctors worked well through the night to save the young child's life. Now this young girl, some eleven years and twenty one surgeries later, with some major medical failures in between, would soon become my roommate. Life did have its unusual twists. I found great excitement in relating to my friends about the newspaper article and of Sheila's talents. Susan was fascinated that even though Sheila and I hadn't met at that point, it seemed as if I already knew her. The newspaper article was complete with a profile view of Sheila playing the piano, her other accomplishments like water skiing, graduating from school for the deaf and blind and even her ability to drive a car, which I always added as my own personal joke. I loved to get a reaction from those who were taken off guard by the thought that Sheila could drive as well.

For the first time in what seemed to be my endless childhood, there was an area of promise and hope in my life. I was able to visit Mama on my own terms and seeing Papa was just the tag along without the consequences. I could now walk away physically from that situation and my future objective would be to eventually do it in my mind as well. The childish games of disassociation which I had used, appeared by that time to be a little immature and rather clumsy. Even though Papa still gave me those knowing looks when he was around, I could retreat at will to the places of safety I had created many years before. All that I was interested in was, that in a matter of months I would be relocating to a 'woodsy' area called Tigerville, South Carolina and leaving Abbeville behind. I would still have the association of woods and wounds lingering in my memory, but there would be at least two hours between me and the grandfather who had abused me and that thought gave me much relief.

I was rather amused by the names of some of our small towns, like Due West, South Carolina. This was where Barry and his fiancé, Laura, would live after their marriage. Barry was a student at Erskine

College and had met her there shortly after his internship had ended at Congressman Dorn's office. The question in my mind was, why name a town after a direction even though logically speaking it had to be due west of somewhere. Then there was Ninety Six whose zip code ended in the forbidden 666. It never occurred to me that Abbeville my hometown or Calhoun Falls was also unique in that each small town, even though it bordered others, was culturally different from the rest and had its own prejudices. I despised the air that each large town would assume in its attempt to make it known that certain people were better than others because of their social graces and station in life.

In the midst of my fascination for the origin of town names I was pleased to know that ours had such a rich historical background. Not many people could claim to live in a town where the first meeting of the confederacy took place. The rich origins of Abbeville were seen around and about a house called 'The Stark House'. There two sisters entertained the Northern generals and probably also served them crumpets and tea while they discussed what their strategy would be to win the 'War Between the States'.

I could not fathom how any state could fight against another because one was brave and daring enough to free its slaves, which in my opinion should never have been an issue in the first place. I know now that no one person owns another and man's inhumanity to man had only brought a trail of blood and bigotry which touched the lives of everyone in the United States, not just the four corners of Abbeville, where I felt so much of the hatred had begun with the acts of the KKK.

Although I still could not recall the despicable act against the innocent black man that bleak night in the woods behind my grandparent's house, I was keenly aware of an overriding ethos of disunity and corruption. Contempt breeds hatred and it strongly influenced my family. I was at least relieved that the prejudice ended with my grandparents and had not been passed down to my mom, or to me and hoped wouldn't be passed on to any children I may have in the future. These stories would not be ones that I would be eager to share with my blind roommate on winter evenings in the dorm.

I remember my first walk down the corridors of the college dorm. Mama seemed to be making a weird huffing and puffing noise as she insisted on managing the chest alone. Papa, who obviously had come along just for the ride, was smoking a cigarette in the college parking lot. In my mind I had this picture of him blasting off into space as he carelessly stood next to the gas tank of the immaculately kept black Buick. Even though the thought gave me a strange serene feeling, I knew this was something that would not happen in reality. If the wish alone for him to be gone had worked he would have disappeared long before that time. He seemed oblivious to the fact that Mama needed help as well as myself with the luggage I had brought to North Greenville. I would have been okay with his inconsideration in not helping had it not been that it was a lot for Mama and me to carry to the dorm.

That day would mark a new beginning for me; at least it was my hope. Even though the ideal scenario would have been to ride to my college destination accompanied by my mom and dad, I had to suffice with my grandparents instead. We were to be joined later by my parents for a late afternoon reception for families of new students to be able to meet the staff. Even though I was looking forward to this, I, in no way, wanted my grandfather to be a part of it. His money was not contributing to my education and Mama had warned me on several occasions not to tell him that she was paying for the tuition. Again secrets were not anything new in my family and the fact that my college tuition was being paid by my grandmother would just add to the list of things that I couldn't reveal.

We were in my dorm room when Sheila and her parents arrived. My first instinct was to look away when she first walked in. In my wildest imagination I had not expected what I saw and was in no way prepared for it. I knew that Shelia was blind but I had not anticipated the extent of her facial injuries or the damage caused by the accident. I couldn't imagine what she had to go through and although the initial shock was great I realized that any negative reaction on my part would not be acceptable. I realized after meeting Sheila why she had been photographed in profile for the newspaper. On one side there was a glass eye but on the other only an empty socket was visible. My parents had always taught me that even if a person was different from me that it was never right to treat them as if they were. I established almost immediately that the only difference between Sheila and I was the fact that she couldn't see. In my heart I knew that it was right to look far beyond external appearances to see the person inside.

I liked Sheila from the beginning as she was funny, talkative and outgoing. I felt pretty unique and privileged being the only student at college with a blind roommate. Sheila's mom and dad talked freely with me and my grandmother, making me feel more at ease. As exciting as this college experience was going to be and even though I felt ready for it, there was, however, a gnawing feeling in the pit of my stomach that seemed to hit me periodically during the afternoon and I wasn't sure what caused it. Maybe the trigger was seeing Sheila for the first time and the thoughts of all that she had gone through. Alternatively it could have been the ride up to North Greenville with Mama and Papa, but whatever it was I wanted the uncomfortable feeling to go away. I became unusually quiet as the day progressed.

I was glad when my mom and dad arrived for the reception. My grandfather had made himself scarce and only made a brief appearance. It was evident he was bored and not at all happy to be a part of this affair. I tried to focus my thoughts on my new life and the fact that I was now in college and everything could now be different. Within a few short hours the reception was over and my parents and grandparents had left.

I was anxious to get acquainted with Sheila and my other suitemates. Missy, Carla, Sheila and I would be sharing a bathroom. Both Missy and Carla seemed to be very outgoing so the four of us spent the rest of the evening in our room talking, discussing our majors and laughing about all the 'treasures' we had brought for the first semester. Carla commented it would have been much easier to have rented a big moving van, but we realized that being young ladies we had to have practically everything but the kitchen sink when going away from home for any extended period of time. After comparing our individual supplies we discovered with amusement that between the four of us we had duplicated many items which included three record players.

I surprised myself in that I felt so comfortable with those three people that I had just met. Perhaps it was a good sign, indicating that the negativity in my life was about to change, and I would finally experience freedom from the fears and insecurities which had plagued me for so long. It would be great reaching out to new friends without the fear of being hurt. It wasn't yet clear in my mind if my new found freedom and feeling of security arose from the hundred miles separation between me and the town where most of my abuse had taken place. But, whatever the reason, I basked in the fact that I at last felt empowered.

After Missy and Carla went back to their own room Sheila and I stayed up talking until after midnight. I was curious as to how she was able to manage attending college while being blind. She talked freely as if she had known me for years. She said that her mother had basically acted as her eyes until she had gone to a school for the deaf and blind when she was about ten years old. Sheila went on to explain that she had not wanted to go away from home but that her mother had been insistent on her learning how to live comfortably in a sighted world, without being too reliant on others.

At the school for the deaf and blind the staff had taught Sheila to become independent in many ways. She had learned how to adapt to new surroundings, how to arrange her clothes according to color co-ordination and even to count and memorize the number of steps from one location to another. Sheila had a Brailler which was exactly like a typewriter but would type in Braille instead of letters so that she could record and check her work. She was also going to have access to audio books for her college courses. I really enjoyed our conversation and found Sheila a very interesting person to talk with, but we both agreed that with church the following morning it would be wise to get some sleep.

I didn't mind stopping at that point because I wasn't at all anxious to reveal details about my life, and had no plans to tell any forbidden secrets. Even though Sheila had directed the conversation toward me more than once, I found a way of redirecting it back to her and hoped she wouldn't realize I was trying to avoid her questions. It was just refreshing to me being able to learn about someone who, even with insurmountable odds stacked against her, would now be able to function well in college. It all made me ashamed of feeling sorry for myself. I could see how she would be an inspiration to me and others. I was able to view my life, which had seemed so utterly hopeless and pathetic, in a new perspective.

I went to sleep that first night excited and encouraged about the chapter of my life that was about to come. Could this be the new beginning that I yearned for? What might lie ahead? Could I put the past and its secrets behind me? Only time would tell.

The only things which seemed to give me any peace
at that time were the occasions when my classmates and I would
join hands as we chanted out in the candlelit dorm room
at our Friday night séances...

CHAPTER 19

Power of The Occult

It wouldn't be long before I would embark on a new journey, one that had similarities to that which I had previously experienced, especially concerning the dark side of life. It had come like an unexpected whirlwind but it was all related to power, power that I felt I had never possessed over my life before but now, in my estimation, would be miraculously given back to me. It was my mom's wish to have me attend a Christian college and she could never have dreamt that I would have become involved in anything such as I was about to engage in, so soon after I had enrolled at North Greenville. My previous achievements in High School English had entitled me to become a member of the EQV Literary Society and I was excited to receive a letter of acceptance that first week of college. Sheila was also eligible to become a member and we began meeting every two weeks in the room of the sophomore president. It was quite an honor to be a member of this elite group. For one who had always felt very insignificant, I made the most of being part of something special.

I can't answer the question of what possessed me to veer off the path that had been set for me when I began college and why I would choose such a different one, especially in lieu of what had transpired earlier in my life. Having already experienced the fear of the occult and its effect on my emotions it would have been much more sensible to resist, especially since I was old enough to make my own decisions and was not being forced to participate. For whatever reason, the door would be opened through my experimentation and it would change my life drastically. It happened in such a subtle way that it would be many years before I realized the total impact of those actions in my life. My intentions had been good after that very compelling talk my mom had with me upon my return from Maryland. Still deep inside there was a void in my life. It was evident that I was searching and the occult, although not new to me, provided yet another way for me to feel accepted and the enticement of the so called power made it a lot more appealing.

There wasn't a lot of substance to the church that we were attending, in that it seemed to follow a formal type of religious tradition. I felt it was incredibly boring and inflexible and not relevant to my life as a whole. Sheila and I often joked about the possibility of the devil hiding in our bathroom, waiting to pounce on us each Sunday morning and then toss us back into bed so that we missed Sunday school. I have to admit I didn't particularly like the college church. We were required to attend the services but the fact that they weren't the 'fire and brimstone' type, which I had been used to, meant that it was easy for me to let my mind wander. I found myself pretending to take notes of the sermons to keep up appearances but was actually diagramming sentences for my English class.

It was evident that something was missing in my life. I had been able to adjust to college and was fascinated by the fact that I was learning quite a bit about life from Sheila. She was very stable and capable in spite of the fact that she was totally blind. We got along wonderfully, except for the fact that I was known to be a neatness freak and would often tidy up her papers and books, placing them in other locations which would make it extremely difficult for her to retrieve them in time for class. I was reprimanded for that and justly so. I promised her that I would do better about the compulsion to rearrange her possessions.

Sheila was relieved, however, at the fact that I was one of the few people besides her mom who didn't treat her as if she had a handicap. We would be walking along the campus and she would trip and I would make a comment like, "Sheila, are you blind or something?"

What might have seemed like a cruel statement to some people was music to her ears. She thanked me for the joke, which showed that I wasn't feeling sorry for her but was treating her like I would any of my other friends.

The highlight of our week was where some of us gathered in a room belonging to one of our group of friends. It didn't take long for our room to become the magnet for this get-together. We were blessed with an over abundance of homemade cookies sent to me by my grandmother and my collection of music was outstanding. It seemed nothing had changed with the fact that my grandmother continued to shower me with gifts on a regular basis. It wasn't the music or cookies alone that attracted large numbers to our room but something far more sinister. Sheila and I had an unusual ability to entertain people with our ESP and other mind games. None of us had meant to get as deeply involved with this aspect of the occult until we bought an Ouija Board. At the time it seemed an innocent enough activity. It was just a game; something different and something to occupy our time on Friday evenings at college.

Our evenings became ones of lighting candles, sitting in a circle holding hands and having séances, at first calling back the spirits of our dead pets. Everyone found this to be more amusing than anything else, but as we began to sink deeper and deeper into the trances that we put ourselves into, there was an aura of intrigue and suspense as the Ouija board provided us with a gateway to another dimension. I was already familiar with this dimension but was reluctant to mention it to any of my friends. The fact that I was a part of something much bigger than myself was in itself a solace even though the bigger thing didn't include my friends. I was still able in my mind to send my body to different locations, a fact that I would not relate to anyone, even Sheila, although we were getting a lot closer as the days progressed.

I remember a particular incident while in a trance one Friday evening where I closed my eyes and felt like a giant molecule in space and envisioned myself with immense power. This reminded me of times when I was younger, in the bedroom at my grandparent's house, except for the fact that in these particular trances I was an epitome of power. It gave me a strange sensation. This had also happened in my Sunday School class at the First Baptist Church after one of our very intense nights in the woods. It was on this occasion that I had in my mind created 'Max' the ultimate of giants. I could still see him in my mind's eye breaking off tall pine trees as if they were match sticks, while he twisted and turned through the briars and branches on his rescue missions. In Max's hand was a tiny hypodermic needle and although he said nothing I knew the injection was intended for me. This was apparently how I would get my power. It was an ancient potion I had once read about, introduced by early Indians and it was said to make one immortal. If my thoughts were to conjure up something to protect me I must assuredly not forget the most important ingredient.

College wasn't particularly easy and I was struggling in the Chemistry class. It wouldn't hurt any of us to have had a giant to hang around the campus. I knew that telling Sheila or any of our friends about Max would not have been wise. Besides, this giant belonged to me and to my knowledge he wouldn't be doing anything for anyone but me. That is what I had grown to learn about those parts of me that had been created through the years. Although I didn't understand anything about them or much about their character, I knew that they were places of safety and the fact that they were created by my mind didn't affect their authenticity.

I had not been use to studying as much as required in order to achieve decent College grades and the fact that I was headed for an unsatisfactory grade in several of my subjects didn't help. Mama was putting a lot of pressure on me to improve and as she explained, this was all she was living for; to see me finish college. She and Papa began visiting most weekends and I became frantic. I had felt that college would get me away from that environment, not make it become prominent in my life again.

Had I instinctively created another dimension through the occult and, if I had, did this place differ from that of disassociation because of the element of power involved? My abuse had been about power and subconsciously my salvation seemed to be about an alternative to this. Had I thought about this spiritually at the time I would have seen clearly the atonement of Jesus Christ. All that I knew was, that having to see my grandparents on weekends had not been in my plan of attending college out of town. This seemed all too familiar to me; and especially since the weekends were involved. I was thankful that there was no way either of them could stay overnight. Just having to sit across from my grandfather at dinner on Saturday afternoon was traumatic enough.

Again, as I had done as a young girl, I looked forward to Friday evenings as I once had with my mom in our tiny one bedroom house on Mrs. Fuller's property. It was now replaced by a dorm room, candlelight and soft whispers as our group called upon the deceased to appear in some form. The flickering of the candles gave way to eerie gasps as the waves of a cold wind would sometimes blow past us. To us this was no different than telling ghost stories by the campfire but it was much more serious in that we were continually opening the door to the enemy of our souls. At the time I understood very little about the destructiveness of our actions and how it would affect our lives later on.

My college classes were getting progressively difficult. The pressure that my grandmother was putting on me to succeed seemed to be taking its toll. She called constantly to check up on me and although I was spending time studying, my concentration wasn't what it needed to be. Sheila seemed to be sailing through all of her classes while I would end up taking 'No Doze', a stimulant, to keep me awake long enough to cram for chemistry tests and other difficult subjects. My grades were not all that high in my Spanish class either and so this was a concern to me. I was still excelling in English, however, which had always been my strongest subject. I could still hear Mama's words ringing in my ears, "All I am living for is that you finish college." I had never wanted to disappoint anyone and especially the one who was paying for my education.

The only things which seemed to give me any peace at that time were the occasions when my classmates and I would join hands as we chanted out in the candlelit dorm room at our Friday night séances. Sheila and I had progressed to another level where the two of us could join hands and participate in ESP, communicating numbers secretly concealed on a sheet of paper. The girls who attended our sessions were amazed at the feats we could achieve using the power of the mind. This wasn't anything new to me because I had being doing this for a long time. I had surmised that perhaps the reason Sheila was so proficient in this area was the fact that she was blind and had therefore developed another sensory perception that others didn't possess. At that time it didn't occur to me that we were deeply involved in witchcraft. All I did know was that it gave me a great sense of power. That power was beginning to control me in ways I had not anticipated.

I still enjoyed my Music classes and like English was excelling there and not having any particular problems. Still there was a gnawing feeling of anxiety within me but I somehow did not relate it in any way to the Friday night activities which we continued to indulge in. I was having some significant nightmares and would wake up some nights in a cold sweat, much the same way I had as a child at my grandparent's house. There would be times when I could actually view myself outside my body. Even though I was not being abused at that time in my mind's eye I could still see a tiny child lying on her bed screaming. I was having many flash backs, things that I couldn't understand, like running through the woods for example. Much of the stress I suffered at college could have been attributed to these things; at least I thought so at the time. It didn't occur to me that my extra-curricular activities could be the root of my problems.

One day in desperation I stopped by Mrs. Crane's room, our dorm leader, and asked if I could talk with her. She could see that I was very distressed. I of course didn't relate any of what was going on, as far as our séances were concerned. I knew that this type of activity would never be permitted in a Christian college. By this time I was addicted to the excitement it brought me and to the attention that I was getting by being able to perform feats which were so astounding to others. This made me feel both important and significant. I didn't want to give it up. Mrs. Crane informed me that there was a counselor at one of the large churches in Greenville who was on the Board of Directors at the college, and that if my parent's agreed I would be given the opportunity to go and talk with him. I felt desperate enough to do anything, especially since I had been having the nightmares occurring more frequently. She said I clearly appeared to be depressed and that talking to him might help me sort out the conflicts I was encountering.

I agreed to let her call my parents. My mother didn't hesitate to give her permission. From past experiences I am sure she was concerned that I might again start self abusing, so the appointment was set for me to meet with the counselor. The last thing I wanted to do was to let my grandmother down and to fail. I had always been taught that excellence was the most important goal in life. I was still trying to keep all the shoes straight so to speak, much as I had tried to do as a young girl to avoid punishment. Now I was doing the same thing, except on a larger scale. It was overwhelming.

My first appointment with the counselor at the church didn't go very well. I felt as if I had shut down and it seemed that all the questions he asked, I either couldn't remember or was just unwilling to open up with any suitable answers. I mainly said what I felt he wanted to hear and that I was in college, under pressure, and just needed to make some adjustments to the new environment. He asked very little about my background and for that I was glad. I didn't want to delve into anything concerning the past. We had several sessions before the Christmas break and he told me that we would continue after I returned from the holidays. Amazingly, even with all that turmoil in my life, I had managed to pass all of my classes but with only a C grade in Chemistry and Spanish.

I wasn't particularly looking forward to Christmas as I would miss my friends at college, especially Sheila. She and I had had become very close friends. We exchanged our Christmas gifts before leaving for the holidays and we vowed not to reveal to anyone about our Friday night meetings. They were to be our secret, a pattern of life which had become well established with me.

The trip back to the college seemed short in lieu of the fact that I would soon be dead. I had no fear. This was the only solution to my dilemma and I was about to carry it out...

CHAPTER 20

Dark Intentions

The Christmas break seemed to pass by quickly and on January 3rd we would be starting classes again. I had hoped my time at home would give me a break from the stress of my studies. My mom and dad seemed to be happy to have me home with them and the only really difficult day was the annual Christmas morning breakfast visit from my grandparents. This had become a tradition for Mama and Papa to make their early morning stop at our house where my mom would prepare her fluffy scrambled eggs, crisp bacon, and 'out of this world' biscuits made from scratch. No one else except my grandmother could create such culinary delights. I think both of them could even make Spam taste appetizing although I couldn't recall either of them attempting to do so. I remember eating it one time and decided then that Spam would only be included on my list of foods if I was starving and had no alternative.

For the second semester I had signed up for the tennis team at college as I felt the exercise would benefit me. It seemed that all I had managed to do over the holidays was to add a few extra pounds from the cookies, fruit cake and delicious meals. It was difficult to resist them because they were much tastier and varied than the bland food from the college cafeteria.

Even though my parents were glad to have me home for a few weeks and I enjoyed being with my sister and family, I still had this gnawing feeling of dread inside when I had to be around my grandfather. He remained silent for most of the time they were visiting but I still stayed as far away from him as I could without drawing too much attention to my presence or my actions. The entire family had been invited to Aunt Ruth's and Uncle Bombie's house on Christmas Eve where we always exchanged gifts. It was amusing to watch how items that we had given as gifts to other family members, several years before, were now returned to one of us, often still in the same package. Bonnie and I snickered as we watched Daddy open a tie rack that we had given to Uncle Bombie the year before. Our gifts were usually 'fresh' as we called them. Those were the gifts that we hadn't recycled to give out several years later.

With the Christmas break over, I was preoccupied with many negative thoughts as I made my way back to North Greenville. I observed the houses along the way, wondering about the families who lived in them. What were their stories and where did they go for comfort on lonely nights? Were there young girls who felt as desperate as I did? I would never know answers to questions like these. My depression increased with every mile we traveled and as I approached the college itself my anxiety increased also. I felt so much was dependent on my success at college and yet all that I actually felt proficient in was my ability with ESP and being able to contact the dead on our Friday evening sessions. These acquired skills would most certainly not have been on my family's list of expectations for me.

Sheila was there when I arrived and seemed eager to tell me about her Christmas vacation. My mom didn't stay long after she dropped me off except to help me with my luggage. She gave me a warm hug and kisses and told me to study hard so that everyone could be proud of me. My heart sunk realizing that I would once more be back in the dreaded Chemistry class as well as continuing my studies in Spanish. I had never been good at foreign languages. For example, in high school Latin, all I had managed to retain was the Lord's Prayer. At that time the 'God of the Pasture' seemed so far away although I could still remember that particular afternoon where He had revealed Himself very vividly. It was amazing how particular scenes would stand out in my mind while yet others remained neatly tucked away in my reservoir of memories so keeping me safe from their devastating grip.

Days became weeks and the weeks became months. My depression did not subside. Thoughts of suicide plagued me almost on a daily basis. I finally admitted this to the therapist I was seeing at the church in Greenville. He insisted that I needed to make a contract with him promising that I wouldn't do anything to harm myself. Even though I had complied with his wishes the thoughts of ending it all were always present with me. Even our Friday night sessions delving into the occult had begun to lose their appeal and were by now mundane to me and my friends became aware something was very wrong.

Sheila kept questioning me about my mood swings but I just attributed it to the extra demands being made on me in the Chemistry and Spanish classes and the effects of taking the stimulant 'No Doze' in order to stay awake at night. The fact that I had been on them for months made it difficult to sleep on weekends. Sheila kept warning me that the pills were only meant to be used occasionally and not every single night. "Not everyone is a genius like you Hilly, "I snapped. "I'll let that go Cooper this time since I believe you are under a lot of stress," she quickly replied. We joked later about how we had called each other by our last names. We didn't usually stay angry for long, even though we did at times get on each other's nerves.

It had also reminded me of another occasion, the one time when Sheila asked for a 'No Doze' tablet so she could stay up all night to study for a mid-term exam. I reminded her that the taking of stimulants like that were not supposed to be good for you. She laughed at me, her hypocritical roommate that night, so instead of giving her 'No Doze' I gave her two aspirins. The next morning she commented on how well they had worked. I gingerly said, "Would have worked better if you had a headache because those were aspirins." This was the first time that Sheila had actually become angry with me since coming to North Greenville. She said almost in tears, "For a person who has never treated me as if I was blind, you took advantage of me last night." She also added that I wouldn't have dared to try that with a sighted person. She was right and I did apologize. She graciously accepted my apology, but then that was Sheila's personality. I had been wrong to trick her in such a manner.

Sheila sailed through her classes and it made me often feel ashamed that I, being a sighted person, had so many problems studying. Even with her limitations, she was maintaining almost a 4.0 GPR. I was amazed at the courage she had and her determination to not let what had happened to her in the past affect her future. There were many times when I felt like a failure in comparison to her because my struggles were so great and most of my days were ones of despair and depression, and would finally turn into desperation.

I constantly poured condemnation on myself in regard to the one thing that my grandmother wanted and was living for and that was to see me finish college. It seemed the harder I tried the more frustrated I became. My frequent question to myself was to ask if I had the ability to do anything right. Somehow I could still recall that water stain on the top of the trunk that had once housed all of my doll's beautiful clothes. Did my soul bear a similar indelible stain as a result of my past mistakes? On Sundays I sat numbly in the church services wondering if God could be in the building and if He was, how He could possibly want anything to do with the vile person that I felt I had become.

The one thing that bothered me more than anything else was the fact that there were so many things that I couldn't remember about my childhood. There were gaps that seemed more like bad dreams and for the most part these seemed to crumble before my eyes when I tried to think about them. I would sometimes wake up in the dorm room in a cold sweat, thinking I was still at my grandparent's house. There were times I would wake Sheila up and then would feel badly about it, especially if I knew she had an early class the next day.

My emotional stability had decreased to an alarming level. I was still seeing the counselor in Greenville. It was difficult to talk to him, especially about not being able to remember certain things concerning my childhood. I still had blank spots during the day and would periodically find myself sitting on a bench on campus, not remembering how I got there. What if I was declared mentally insane like an aunt of mine? I recalled my grandmother making remarks about her many times and the fact that mental illness ran in our family. Was I doomed to that same fate?

My difficulty in being able to sleep at night was getting worse and any call from my grandmother, asking about my grades, would send me spiraling into a panic attack. Mama was relentless in her demands for my success in college. She reminded me of how much she was sacrificing and the fact of how much money she had already lost in my short lived desire to become an airline stewardess. The fact that it wasn't her idea made this career even more bizarre in her eyes. "How can you possibly think of going off to another state and fly on a jet from one place to another?" she quizzed impatiently one afternoon, shortly after I had finished high school.

She finally agreed to pay for the correspondence course and my signed contract with Weaver Airline School would assure me a job upon its completion. I was required to lose twenty five pounds which I glibly thought would make me attractive enough to be a stewardess. I wasn't sure what the big issue was unless they felt that my extra weight would make the plane crash. I remember the embarrassment I felt when the representative came to our house for my interview and asked me to walk in front of him and to turn around. I felt like one of my uncle's prize pigs on display as it was pondered on which was fat enough to be chosen for his last truck ride to be butchered.

My ordeal was different in that the representative of the school said that even though I was relatively attractive, their guidelines called for slender young ladies and the weight must be lost before I could be accepted at the airline school. My self-image was not at its highest level anyway and his remark was yet another crystallizing event, making me feel that I had to look a certain way to be acceptable. This was another bitter root that would take many years to pull out of my garden of negative, self condemning thoughts.

The next few days were a blur. I remember the college van taking me into town for my meeting with the counselor. Because of my mental state Mrs. Crane, the dorm monitor, had suggested I see him on that Friday. As soon as I mentioned suicide it was then that he said he would call my parents to ask them to pick me up at college. My face was blank, but as I sat in his office that day my mind had already devised a plan. I would not be alive when they arrived. I had bought a large bottle of sleeping pills a few weeks before and was about to use them.

There was no way I would go home to face the humiliation of being a mental case. It made me wonder how my biological father had felt right before he took his life. In my mind my life was already over and although I would have no control over this aspect of what would transpire, I wanted my tombstone to read, 'She had no purpose. She just lived and failed.' The trip back to the college seemed short in lieu of the fact that I would soon be dead. I had no fear. This was the only solution to my dilemma and I was about to carry it out.

It was late Friday evening when I arrived back at the college. Sheila was anxious to find out how my session went. My answer was a short, "Everything's going to be fine." as I lay across the bed in an exhausted heap. She didn't question me anymore, apparently sensing that I didn't want to discuss anything further. By this time she had grown accustomed to my mood swings and usually made allowances for them. My thoughts focused on how easy it would be to walk to the sink right outside our bathroom door, open the bottle of pills, take them one by one and then lie down on the bed and wait to die. It wasn't as if I would have to hide to do it. Sheila wouldn't be able to see my actions but would assume I had just dropped off to sleep, thereby allowing plenty of time for the pills to do their 'work'. There was something, however, that I hadn't counted on that night, which was Sheila's incredible ability to perceive when there was something wrong. She had told me many times that when a person loses one of their five senses that God replaces that loss with added ability to sense danger.

My half glass of water sat on my night table. I had just swallowed the last of a whole bottle of sleeping pills. I suddenly felt Sheila sit down on the side of my bed. She shook me and told me that Mrs. Crane had informed her that my parents were on the way to pick me up and that I should get packed. I sleepily told her that wouldn't be necessary because all I wanted to do was to just go back to sleep. I felt serenely calm. In my mind I knew that everything would soon be over. Now, as I relate the story of that night, I realize that I wasn't sure then if she had detected something in my voice that was alarming to her. But for whatever reason, Sheila was apparently prompted to go and get help. What transpired after that I don't really remember but I do vaguely recall faces, people talking, and passing lights above my head as I was rolled in on a gurney to a room where doctors and nurses began working to save my life.

If I could have had one wish that night it would be to never open my eyes again, but they did open, and there standing by my bedside was a man who appeared to be quite elderly; at least that was my impression on seeing him for the first time. He wore glasses, had a kind face and his hair was almost completely white. Ironically he was introduced to me as Dr. Charles White and he was a psychiatrist. It was apparent my plan had failed. Here I was still alive and suddenly thrust into a situation of having to explain my behavior again, this time to a total stranger. My mom was nowhere in sight. Could it be that she had abandoned me again, in much the same way I felt she use to do when leaving me at Mama and Papa's house?

My memory of the trip to the hospital was enclosed in a complete fog. Everyone around me seemed hurried and excited in contrast to the way I felt. My plans were sure and set in emotional concrete. I simply did not want to live. There was no way that I could make my grandmother, mom or anyone else in my family for that matter, understand how badly I was feeling. They couldn't appreciate that my goals weren't being achieved, nor how strongly I felt the 'other side', meaning the dark side; had somehow persuaded me to adopt their point of view. In my understanding, if the light was unable to illuminate the truth, then perhaps the darkness would be able to cover all the secrets I had been trying to hide since I was four years old.

Everything that I would believe about family, or even come close to believing, would be challenged in the months ahead, as well as those unexpected things that had seemed to follow me throughout my life. My dreams had become splinters of giant 'might have beens', or at least that was the way my depressed mind was viewing the situation since my failed suicide attempt. To suddenly wake up in a hospital, vaguely remembering how I had gotten there was frustrating, to say the least, as well as the fact that I felt I had stumbled into a geriatric nightmare. The doctor sitting beside me was a very elderly man, or at least that was the way he appeared to me. At the age of eighteen, anyone over twenty five was considered old by me and my peers. I was somewhat relieved that it would be many years before I would reach that milestone in life. His very presence made me uncomfortable as he reminded me of my grandfather.

At that time, however, there were more plaguing dilemmas, like how I would manage to catch up with my college assignments. In my more stable moments, when I was able to reason, I kept asking myself why God had allowed me to survive and also dwelt on the fact that I wasn't even able to get the suicide right. Was I really that much of a failure?

Dr. White had called both my mom and dad in for a consultation. He explained to them that each person possessed a certain level of emotion that could fluctuate. At times, depending on the stress level, the emotions could periodically take a nose dive that would plunge the patient into severe depression. He informed my parents that the real danger was when the emotions went below a certain level and remained there. Dr. White said that this is what had happened to me and without help it was unlikely that I would come out of that depression.

His advice to my parents was to give permission for me to be placed in the State Hospital for a period of time. I was present when he discussed this with them. My mom's voice noticeably broke as she struggled to remain composed. I just stared at a book on Dr. White's desk and listened intently as Mother questioned him about my treatment and any other possible options. There was only one, but when it was mentioned my mom vehemently discounted it and said, "Under no circumstance will I agree to her having shock treatment!"

My mind immediately recalled a documentary I had seen which related how a mentally ill person would be placed on a table, strapped down and a black cork placed in their mouth. A local anesthetic would be given and then electrical charges would be administered. I had only been in Greenville Memorial Hospital for a few days when a woman there gruesomely described her experience with 'electric shock' and her fear of not getting the black cork securely placed in her mouth before the procedure began. As I sat in one of the big leather chairs in the psychiatrist office at the hospital, accompanied by my parents, I was convinced my next stop would be a mental institution. Fear consumed me as it had done many times before. I began to search for that place deep within my mind where I could find a secure solace; a place to hide; a place where I could again take the secrets and bury them. Maybe this time that place would be in a padded cell.

Although my thought processes were being altered, I possessed enough rationality to actually believe that I was in the hell that I had envisioned as a child on the bed at my grandparent's house...

CHAPTER 21

Humiliation, Horror and Hopelessness

The thoughts of an institution were more than sobering for a young girl who was eighteen but also necessary for that same young girl who had a few weeks earlier sought to end her life by taking a bottle of sleeping pills. The time lapse between leaving my college dorm to watching my mom walk out of those locked doors at the state hospital seemed almost instantaneous. I vaguely remembered our pastor driving my mom and myself to the place called Bull Street in Columbia, South Carolina. The institution had quite a reputation with nicknames like, the 'End Of The Road Motel', 'Nut City' and other derogatory opinions held by people with a limited view of such places. Nevertheless it wasn't a place I wanted to be but at that point in my life I had no choice. I knew that, if I refused, my parents would send me anyway because they had made it explicitly clear that they would not stand around and watch me destroy my life. Even though my mom was use to my erratic behavior, she knew that this suicide attempt was a very close call and was very serious about me getting some help.

Dr. Smith had done all he could do and his advice to my mom was for me to get some very serious in-house counseling at a hospital that could help me as well as keep me safe. He said that after a week in a closed ward at the state hospital, I would be placed in a cottage, where there would be other college students. At the beginning the thoughts of being locked up were very frightening. Even though I had locked myself in the prison of my mind many times, this was different. I had never been near a mental institution before, let alone being a resident in one, and those rising thoughts of the aunt who had gone off the deep end were ever present in my memory on the long ride to Columbia that day. My mom sat very solemnly in the front seat as Preacher Benjamin drove us those fifty odd miles to the state hospital. I could hear her stifling her tears as she dabbed her eyes periodically with a tissue.

I knew she was suffering about as much as I was mentally because I had heard her crying the night before as she packed my bags. I pretended to watch television but my interest was not at all on the program being broadcasted that particular night. My life was changing drastically as by the following mid-day, I would be committed to a mental institution.

As I relate this portion of the story there are incidents that stand out in my mind concerning the State Hospital. The memories, considering the fact that my stay was only a month, were limited but those that I had were both intense and crude. This was a crystallizing event resulting in me never again feeling secure in a professional environment where there was supposed to be safety and help.

It was late afternoon before all the papers were signed, and I had been introduced to the three doctors, who were assigned to my case. I was suddenly important enough to warrant three doctors! This would be a first but I was not impressed. Neither was I impressed with the requirement, in the presence of a nurse, to remove all of my clothes and stand in front of her as she searched me for any drugs or weapons which could be used for self harm. The body cavity search was even more humiliating. It would stand out in my memory for many years.

Mother stayed until I was finally in the ward, wearing men's pajamas that were far too big for me and being told that I would be able to put on regular clothes after the doctor's examination. I didn't look forward to it but then I was looking forward to nothing concerning this experience. I longed to be back at college, sitting on my bed, watching Sheila sweep and wondering how a blind person could be so precise in cleaning our dorm room. My mind quickly brought me back to reality as I watched my mom walk away down the corridors of the ward with the nurse quickly locking the doors behind her. She had given me a swift but firm hug and kiss but didn't look back as she and Preacher Benjamin disappeared from sight.

I was left alone with my thoughts and they became rampant and scary, as you would imagine, for one who had just been committed to a mental institution. The nurses wasted no time in giving me my medicine and placing me in an examining room, where I was to wait for the doctor. After his visit my regular clothes were returned to me and I can remember feeling a bit more comfortable then.

On my first night in the state hospital I was sitting in the recreation room when one of the girls there with us suddenly got up on a chair and reported that every time the TV flickered it would be aliens trying to get in contact with us. I sat there rather dumbfounded and by the time I was approached by another young girl in the cafeteria who asked me if her hamburger was real, I was absolutely determined that I had to get out of that place. My goal was to work at getting out, no matter how many doctors I would have to deceive in order to do so.

It was bad enough on days when we would have to go from one place to another for various classes and meetings and to have to listen to the horrible screams coming from the building, which others referred to as the ones with padded cells, on the way. These were where those labeled lunatics stayed. I hated that term although it was mentioned quite often. I was horrified at the thought of being placed in one of those rooms. Another incident was in church on the first Sunday morning. Although we weren't required to go to services, I chose to because I hated being in the locked ward that first week and I would have done anything to get out of it. In the middle of the service a girl let out a blood curdling scream, one that I would have guessed came from someone who was possessed by demons, thinking of stories which I had read about. That was my first and last appearance in church for the whole time I was at the hospital.

Although I had not needed to disassociate for quite some time, there arose a situation while at that institution which made it necessary for me to do so, in order to survive the anguish of what took place there. A new pocket of hidden memory would soon lodge deep into my mind as I later lay on a dirty cot in the basement of an old building at the State Mental Institution. I had met another college student and his name was Michael. We immediately liked each other and spent break time sitting on one of the benches in the grounds, talking. One afternoon we went walking into an area that was off limits to patients. We had unknowingly broken hospital rules.

The next afternoon I left my small unlocked cottage with one of the orderlies who was to take me to where my cottage mates were doing crafts. I thought it odd that the route he was using wasn't the usual one. He said that someone wanted to talk to me about disobeying hospital rules. He led me to one of the older buildings, down some steps into the basement area. There we were met by another orderly in a small room with nothing but a cot in the center with dirty blankets thrown over it. I knew instinctively what was about to take place. The pain and humiliation was horrible and I again had to retreat into those secret places in my mind.

After the ordeal was over they took me upstairs to what looked like a hospital room. I was weak and crying from trying to fight off my assailants. They kept saying that I had better be quiet or else I would get more of the same. At that point it didn't take much effort to force me on to a table where they strapped my hands and feet tightly with leather straps. They forced my mouth open and placed some sort of rubber stopper in it.

I could remember the two guys arguing and one kept saying, "My God, you're going to kill her man." The other cursed and said, "I know what I'm doing because I've seen it hundreds of times." Then they attached wires to my head. I couldn't move and I couldn't scream. I wanted to die but the only thing I knew how to do was to go beyond the hiding place in my mind. This time my mind venture wasn't successful because of what was to follow.

Suddenly the most horrendous, excruciating pain went through my head and I could see swirling colors like a kaleidoscope. The colors were vivid but I kept thinking that colors weren't supposed to hurt. These did, however, and the pain began to escalate to such an intense level that I felt any second my head would surely explode into millions of tiny pieces. If my mind could have had the capacity to think beyond that, I would have realized that I was having some type of seizure because my head was convulsing wildly from side to side.

Although my thought processes were being altered, I possessed enough rationality to actually believe that I was in the hell that I had envisioned as a child on the bed at my grandparent's house. Then blackness enveloped me and when I later awoke my head hurt very badly. I didn't know why. It would be at least forty years before I would remember the events of that afternoon. From that time, however, I developed an abnormal fear of hospitals and doctors in white coats and, although it seemed irrational, I was unable to remember the events that caused it until much later.

Years later I returned to that hospital and walked the grounds there and stood in front of that old building, no longer in use. It was a towering reminder of the things that had taken place there. I wept that day, not just for what had happened to me but what probably had happened to others as well. One thing I did know that afternoon in May, as I revisited my place of horror, the nightmare was over and I could finally be free from it.

*I just felt that being in love and entering marriage
was inevitably the answer to all the uncertainties that had plagued
me through the years….*

CHAPTER 22

Whirlwind Relationship

Together with the fact that my college days and thirty long nights in a mental institution were forever behind me, I now had a new perspective. The reality of this perspective was that I really didn't know how to spend the rest of my life. My initial thoughts of being an airline stewardess were now a thing of the past and upon reflection I had to admit it wasn't the fact that I was about thirty pounds overweight that kept me from attaining my goal. I would not be serving coffee, tea and bagged peanuts upon completing the Weaver Airline correspondence course simply because I was, what pre-teens referred to as being 'chicken'. The thoughts of parachuting out of a jet with failed engine were not at all appealing. It was easier to admit I was afraid to go to the dentist, with the crude black instruments hanging menacingly around the dental chair like something straight out of a monster movie, than it was to say that I had a morbid fear of flying.

It was now time to accomplish something. Danny had long been out of the picture so I could now think of a new boyfriend and possibly marriage. Some of my friends were already married and they seemed to be happy. The really difficult task in finding someone in the small town of Abbeville was the fact that most of the boys, who I had attended school with, were more like brothers.

We had hung out together, gone to the Highway 25 drive-in movie, sometimes carrying a few extra passengers in the trunk in order to slip in without paying the full fee. We had shared secret dreams and hopes on lazy summer days but I couldn't imagine any one of those in our group who I would ever think about marrying. Considering the fact that I had not been home long from a mental institution, it was hard to conceive that any of them would be interested in even talking to me, much less marrying me.

My mind quickly recalled the statement that was made to me during my first shopping trip after getting home. A former school mate had come up to me at the drug store and said that she didn't know that there was something wrong with my mind. I just stood there stunned, unable to respond or answer her. I walked away still hearing the words as if they were piercing my heart. I would once again have to send this memory to the hiding place in my mind, that emotional vault for words or phrases I couldn't handle.

Now I was finally back at home, apparently in one piece, but yet in many pieces in my mind. Coming back to a small hometown was not the ambition of most young people, but to one who still possessed much insecurity it was the only option for me at that point in my life. There was nothing to do in the small town of Abbeville but get a secretarial job at a local factory and buy a brand new blue '66 Mustang', so that was exactly what I did. I could now again cruise 'The Ranch' in Greenwood on weekends and wake up to the sound of the lawn mower on Saturday mornings, leave my un-cashed checks on my dresser until time for my car payment or insurance and eat my mom and dad's food.

My grandmother was happy I was home and was hoping that I had changed enough to once more begin visiting on the weekends. Deep down inside I realized that those days were over forever and the only times that I would be sitting at their table would be with the family on special occasions. Upon buying my new Mustang I gingerly rode out into the country making every effort to not go inside the house. It gave me a buzz to blow the horn and then watch the expression on Mama's face as she saw the 'adult' who was before her. I was no longer that curly haired little girl anymore although much residue of her still lurked in the shadowed recesses of my mind. I felt a sense of liberation in knowing that I had the choice to reverse out of the driveway that day. As Mama and Papa stood there, I watched safely from a distance while sniffing my new car smell aroma and sensing a gentle breeze of freedom flow over me.

I was basking in the ease that having little responsibility gave me. I was still required to attend church as long as I resided at my parent's house and even this wasn't my biggest priority at the time, I basically knew that I had it made. There was no rent to pay, my laundry was being done because I was working full time and on weekends I would cruise the Ranch with my friends. In the midst of enjoying the company of my single girl friends, the images of people screaming out of barred windows had finally become less prominent in my mind.

There would be one Sunday night that would change my life forever. It started out after church when several of my friends were 'cruising' about town. I was proudly sporting my '66 Mustang 'when suddenly we found ourselves being followed by a car and as we made the turn on the Abbeville 'square' we noticed two young men inside. I immediately made the observation that we needed to ignore them because we hadn't recognized the car. With Abbeville being a small town we usually knew the cars and their occupants. We made the turn that would take us by the local restaurant in which most of the young people hung out.

I was with one of my friends, Joan Dellinger who for a time had attended North Greenville. She left in the middle of the school year a little while before I had my nervous breakdown. I was later to find out that it was because she had been interested in Danny, the young man that my mother had forbidden me to date. Although it at first had upset me, I was to later find out that she was doing me a favor. By then I realized my mom was right in her decision that Danny wasn't suitable for me. Joan and I had been able to salvage our friendship even though initially there were some hard feelings. I found it amazing how strong friendships were during those days and how, even in the midst of quarrels, we were able to patch things up quickly. .

Joan's interest with Danny hadn't been long term and soon we were back having slumber parties, popping corn and having 'taffy pulls' way into the middle of the night. Now on this particular

Sunday evening we parked at the Kum Back and were immediately approached by the two guys in the car that had followed us. As we were placing our order for curb service, they walked up to the car. There standing by my Mustang were two young men, one dressed in a white sailor suit and the other in regular street clothes. The sailor was approximately six feet tall and quite handsome while his friend was about my height but equally as attractive. I mused to myself that they resembled the cartoon characters, 'Mutt and Jeff.'

It didn't take us long to find out their names and the fact that they were both stationed in Charleston and the short guy was engaged to a local girl. Joan hinted to me while they were placing their order that the sailor was hers. I quickly replied, "No way, Joan." We both laughed but by the end of our conversation I had given Gary, the handsome young man dressed in white, my phone number. He said he would call me the next time he was in town, which turned out to be approximately two weeks later.

Our date turned into a whirlwind relationship. I thought it very unusual for him to tell me he loved me on our first date but it was obvious that I was ready to hear these words and eight months later at a beautiful wedding at the First Baptist Church we were married. We spent our honeymoon in Orlando Florida and thus began our life together that would last for the next nineteen years.

After a week's honeymoon in Daytona Beach, Florida, I remember so vividly picking up the rest of our wedding gifts from my McGowan Avenue home, before my husband and I officially moved to a small apartment at the end of Magazine Street in Abbeville. This was the same street on which I, as a child, had lived with my mom and grandparents. I had asked to sit in the car as Gary retrieved the last of our prized possessions that had been on display in my parent's living room. Tears slowly trickled down my cheeks as I felt a sense of loss, panic and lack of confidence in my ability to be the kind of wife that I desired to be.

It was evident that I didn't want to show in my emotions how difficult it was for me in leaving home and beginning a new life with someone I had only dated for eight months. Although, like any new bride, I was relatively sure this had to be a 'marriage made in heaven' and so despite my reluctance to accept change, I set out on a quest to be the best wife ever. My goal was to be a testimony to all women setting out on a journey of marital bliss. Those values that had been instilled within me by my mom were ever present and constantly making me aware that excellence was something that I should achieve on a regular basis. These principles which my mom had upheld showed me that even in adverse circumstances dreams could come true.

My years of insecurities and being jealous of my sister seemed to be such a long time ago. I really felt that marriage was going to be different for me. There would still be questions as to whether I would make it this time. I could not afford to entertain thoughts that this chapter in my life would end up like my futile attempt at being an airline hostess, or of never reaching good grades in Chemistry. I just felt that being in love and entering marriage was inevitably the answer to all the uncertainties that had plagued me through the years. Finally I had someone who loved me, who accepted me as I was; faults and all.

It didn't taken me long to realize that marriage was a big adjustment. It wasn't just the tiny apartment where Gary and I lived those first few months that bothered me. It wasn't even the fact that it was so small that our sink was positioned in the living-room rather than the bathroom, and that we didn't have a closet in our bedroom, but just a clothes rack instead. I was reminded of the wardrobe that had sat in the small bedroom at Mrs. Fuller's house which then triggered memories of some of the unpleasant things that had happened in the earlier years of my life. This made my first months of marriage more difficult than they might have been had the memories not been dredged up.

Our furniture was very basic and only a fragment of what would be considered a decent living room suite. When we were told this was a furnished apartment neither of us had a clue that the sofa was going to be made of wood, with no cushions and definitely not something on which we could fall asleep when watching television on a cold December night. Gary and I both found it quite amusing that the bathroom sink had to sit in the living room for lack of space and also that slats of our bed would often crash to the floor in the middle of the night during a sound sleep. We considered these to be minor inconveniences in lieu of the fact that we were in love and could be content anywhere, even in a small apartment, void of sofa cushions, a sink in the bathroom and undersized bed slats.

One thing we had not planned for was an oversized budget. We had both purchased new cars not long before our marriage; a Mustang for me and a Corvair for Gary. Even though this hadn't been a major financial burden while being single, it then became one with the added responsibilities, including rent and utilities, on top of the high automobile payments. We would both have to work very hard for quite some time to compensate for our extravagance in automobiles.

Gary was fortunate that he was able to get a drafting job at Davis and Floyd Engineers in Greenwood and I had put in my application for a job at one of the larger banks in town. My aunt Ruth, who had always had a lot of influence with the 'elite', was able to put a good word in for Gary with Judge Erwin who in turn was friends with Emmit Davis owner of the Engineering Firm. Gary had landed this job even before his discharge from the Navy. It was good to know he would have a job waiting for him after getting out of the service.

Because I had clerical experience at two firms in Abbeville it wasn't difficult for me to get the banking job. Even though my confidence level wasn't at its highest, the fact that I would be in the bookkeeping department took me somewhat out of the public eye and placed me upstairs in a 'tucked away' area, an arrangement which pleased me and brought great relief. There was, however, a down side to being a bookkeeper. It meant long hours recalculating if we were out of balance, and, since we worked very closely with the proof department, there were many evenings that we all sat at a table examining long strips of paper looking for errors. It was even worse at the end of the month when we had to send out statements. Nothing was computerized then and so all checking took a long time.

My pay was approximately sixty three dollars a week while Gary's was at best eighty five. I was salaried so that meant no overtime for the long hours, and there were some evenings where it would be past eleven at night before I would arrive home. One week's pay for the two of us was approximately the total amount of our car payments. This meant that there were some lean days in the first year of our marriage.

Mama was more than happy to help with groceries and other necessities but most of the financial help that she gave came with some form of strings attached. I felt this had been the case for most of my life and to accept help from her would basically give her permission to tell me how to dress, how to act, which friends I could have and even worse make me feel obliged to visit them more often. This put me in a triggering position with Papa. My days of abuse were over but the nightmare still seemed so real every time I walked into their country home. A sullen stillness would come over me, as well as a chill that seemed to seep straight into my bones, as I reluctantly paid my expected visit to the place where I stayed most weekends as a child.

There in the quiet, except for the rumble of the football crowd on television, I knelt quietly and asked Jesus to come into my heart …

CHAPTER 23

Spiritual Awakening

My life was changing fast but my emotions were not. I still went through bouts of depression and intense times of anger and couldn't figure out why. Gary, most of all, didn't understand and how could he? Deep within the recesses of my mind were pictures and images that often woke me in the middle of the night. In my dreams I frequently found myself at my grandparent's house, where I was running, always being pursued by flashes of darkness, like specters on hazy nights. These dreams seemed so real. I wasn't that little girl anymore but in my mind I certainly felt like her.

Within a few months of marriage, Gary realized that driving back and forth to Greenwood for our jobs was a bit taxing, so he decided that if we bought a mobile home and moved closer to our workplaces it would be more economical. He managed our finances well but, we were both reminded, when the car payments came due each month just how irresponsible we had been in purchasing two new expensive cars. Had it not been for my grandmother's bags of groceries, which she brought us most weeks; we would have often gone hungry.

Gary and I decided that we would wait a year before we started a family and so we did. We had married on December 3rd 1966 and by the end of the next year I proudly announced to everyone that we would be having our first child the following September. We were attending Laurel Baptist Church at that time and I remember the excitement of going there and sharing our good news with my closest friends.

I was a bit worried though. I had never been a mother before and often wondered if I would make a good one. I am sure that all parents question themselves in this way, but especially moms. Everyone warned me that I could have morning sickness but, the good news was that, I never did experience that except for one occasion. Gary had an aggravating habit of mixing up odd combinations in the blender. One included canned sardines, catsup, mustard and potted meat mixed together. This particular morning he was in a hurry and asked me if I would prepare his sandwiches. I had already felt a bit queasy upon awakening but all it took was the aroma of Gary's patent mixture to send me running to the bathroom. From then on I made it very plain that he would have to make his own sandwiches whatever the time.

We were all excited about the expected baby and especially my grandmother who busied herself buying extravagant cribs and accessories. She declared this baby would want for nothing, in much the same way as me. Just the thoughts of ever allowing any child of mine to be at their home caused a chill that seemed to penetrate right through my body. Still I remained silent because at that time I had successfully been able to block out most of what had happened to me there. All that remained was a dread, a consuming fear that followed me like a cloud even on sunny days.

I continued to work at the bank, but mathematics had never been my expertise so balancing accounts at the end of a busy day became very frustrating. I would learn in later years that a person is rarely happy doing those things they are not really called to do. I had definitely not been called to be a banker, but at the time my salary did manage to pay some of the bills. In the early days of our marriage everyday chores and financial responsibilities tended to dominate our thinking and spirituality was far from our minds. This all changed on a Sunday in April a few months before our first baby was due.

Gary and I had lunch with my mom and dad. Shortly after dinner mother said she wanted to talk with me. I followed her into the living room leaving Gary and my dad watching a football game. We sat down on the sofa and Mother surprised me with a very unusual request. "Tell me about your experience when you accepted Jesus as your Savior," she asked. Even though I can't recall my exact reaction that day I am sure that I must have responded in a way that seemed to satisfy her, at least for that time. The truth was that deep inside something significant struck me right in the middle of my heart. I knew at that precise time that I had no such personal experience.

I had noticed something different about Mother; even though she had always been a religious person, she was now more passionate about her beliefs than before. She had gone to a place called 'Camp Zion' in Myrtle, Mississippi and something special had happened to her while she was there. She expressed how she now had a real burden for her family and wanted to be certain that each one had asked Jesus into their heart. She related to me that she felt led to go to each member personally and ask them if they really knew Jesus. Besides my Aunt Grace, I was the second one she had approached in this way. After our talk I nervously chewed at my nails and was relieved when Gary was ready to leave somewhat earlier than usual. I chuckled when I realized it was half way through the game and would leave just enough driving time to put him back in front of the television without missing one touchdown.

All the way back to Greenwood that afternoon my thoughts were not on football or even the fact that mother had cooked one of my favorite meals, her famous spaghetti with fresh olives, and tossed salad with homemade croutons. I could only think of the fact that if Gary were to wreck the car on the way home that I might die and end up in hell. I pondered carefully on the fact that a few short months before Gary had told me that he believed as the Baptists did and not those doctrines of his Lutheran upbringing. For the first time in my life I realized that it wasn't about Baptists, Lutherans or any other denomination, but that it was all about Jesus and a relationship with Him. Could it be that I was about to embark on one of my greatest journeys yet?

It was early afternoon when we arrived back home. On the way I had visualized Gary going over the embankment and as I was about to take my last breath a smelly demon from hell was there to escort me on my way to a place of utter darkness and torment. This had been so vivid, that by the time we were home, it seemed that I could not get on my knees fast enough. Gary went back to his football game as I made a quick retreat to the bedroom.

There in the quiet, except for the rumble of the football crowd on television, I knelt quietly and asked Jesus to come into my heart. Even though I didn't understand very much about what I was doing that spring day, there was one thing that I was sure of, and that was that I was lost and needed a Savior. This was the One mother had spoken of so many times; the One who had died for me, that curly haired little girl whose only previous encounter had been with the distant 'God of the Pastures' several times before. On April 28th, 1968 I again met this same God but this time it wasn't a casual meeting like it had been behind my house in a cow pasture. I was assured that He was not going to be that whimsical presence that would be here today and gone tomorrow, as many had done in my life. Although my emotions would many times whisper these lies to me, I found an incredible peace that day.

Although I couldn't explain to Gary what had happened to me because it was all so new, I made plans to attend the evening service at Laurel that night. When the invitation was given, I went down and whispered in the pastor's ear that I was thankful God had saved me and had given me another chance. At the time I was disappointed that he didn't announce it to the church but then later felt a tinge of guilt that maybe my decision had been a fleshly one, and that perhaps I had needed the approval of people more than God. At any rate, I was what the Christian community called saved and my mind pondered the glorious fact that surely my life could only get better from this point.

I finally had something that I could call my own. My first experience in Christianity was even more special than evenings spent with my precious dolls at my grandparent's house when I was a child. This seemed so real, not like the fantasy world that my mind had to create in order to help me survive the horrors of the past. There was something about the concept of God that intrigued me and because of that I was anxious to share with my mom what had transpired that Sunday afternoon as soon as possible. As I look back on this, I cannot recall if my desire to be accepted may have been another motivating factor in coming to Jesus as well as my intense fear of burning forever in that endless fire of hell. Nevertheless I had made a decision and it almost coincided with me becoming a mother for the first time. The last four months of my pregnancy seemed to go slowly as Gary and I waited patiently for the arrival of our firstborn.

Mother was elated when I shared with her the details of my salvation experience. With tear filled eyes she gave me a hug and for a moment, with hands still on my shoulders, instructed me on how she felt I could grow in the Lord. "Hon, you need to stay in the Word. The enemy goes around like a roaring lion and he would love to steal your joy." "Don't let him do that," she spoke sternly but with much love and intent.

I explained that I had already been attending a Bible study at Mrs. Anna Duncan's house, a dear, kind and dedicated lady who attended my church. I always listened intently each time she spoke, and you could see the love of Christ radiating out of her with each statement she made. There was something special about this woman and the spirit that she possessed was similar to the one that Mother displayed. I left each Bible study full of hope and with an inexplicable peace. All this was new to me but I liked it.

Peace was something that I had sought after for years but which had seemed to be an unattainable goal. Now I knew something positive was happening in my life and I longed to share it with others. My stepfather was also excited about my decision to accept Christ. Every time Gary and I visited on Sunday afternoons he made a point of taking me into his study at least once to share some deep spiritual revelation God had given him the week before. I felt that my knowledge of the Bible was inferior to his, and would sometimes become a bit frustrated that he knew so much where I seemed to know so little.

There had been some major changes in my life since April 28th. I began to develop a deep hunger for the Bible. I would read long into the night. I found that some passages in the Old Testament were confusing. Those things that I didn't understand, I would ask Mother or Mrs. Duncan and even my stepfather who, since his salvation at forty years of age, had become an avid student of the Word. He spent most of his extra time studying the Bible or listening to Christian tapes. His library of books included Spurgeon, Watchman Nee, and his all-time favorite, Oliver B. Green.

I was conscientious in keeping a journal of all that God was doing for me and especially what He was showing me in the Bible and how I could apply it to my daily life. There were, however, some uncovered issues that I knew I hadn't yet faced and so treated them in a similar way to those 'secrets' of my childhood. I found myself in the same position of being unable to share with others.. By then, although not still in an abusive situation, the gnawing fear of what might happen to me if I related details of my past sent chills up and down my spine. I was spending virtually no time at my grandparent's house and the only occasions when I felt uneasy was when we had a family dinner there, which had become a rarity. We usually gathered at Mother's house and she would invite Mama and Papa which still made me feel very uncomfortable.

One Sunday afternoon as we ate dinner together at my parent's house I looked up and noticed Papa had this strange glare in his eyes. Then his head began to drop and he turned the deepest color of blue I had ever seen. I couldn't budge from my spot. I just stared at him for what seemed to be an eternity and then blurted out, "What is wrong with him?" My grandmother, who was sitting nearby, jumped up and put her arms around him and cried out, "Oh my God, He is dying! Please don't let him die!" I couldn't handle it any longer. I got up and went into the living room and actually stood there praying that it would be over soon. I could not bring myself to ask for God to spare him. I anticipated news of his death at any moment but about five minutes later someone said he was coming around. Dr. Poliakoff had already been called and he was on his way. This was at a time when doctors made house calls.

While we were awaiting the arrival of the doctor, Gary came in and put his hand on my shoulder, assuring me that Papa was going to be ok. I didn't respond to that but rather stared out of the big picture window until I saw the doctor pull into the driveway. I didn't like my thoughts, because by then I was saved and therefore should have had a different viewpoint. Things were supposed to have changed. I shouldn't have been wishing that Papa would die. The guilt began to sink deeply into my mind, tossing me around like a rag doll and making me feel dizzy, I just wanted to go home.

Dr. Poliakoff didn't stay long but told us the crisis was over and it was possible that Papa had suffered a mini stroke. He told my grandmother to just watch him and take him to the hospital if he had any signs of weakness in his arms or legs. For now he said everything was fine and she should probably just drive him home so he could rest. Thoughts of previous visits to Dr Poliakoff's office made me take a long deep sigh.

I was glad when the day was over. I could not sleep that night and every time I closed my eyes, I visualized Papa as the blue in his face got darker and darker. Whenever I did fall asleep I experienced horrible nightmares, similar to those before where I continued to run through the woods trying to escape my assailant. I could only pray that the next day would be better. I didn't feel worthy to even pray that night because of my actions at Mother's house and the fact that I was actually wishing that Papa would die. What kind of Christian would do such a thing?

I shook my head in disbelief for all the years I had feared this man,
and could only be thankful that the precious little baby sleeping in
the next room would never have to go through what I had...

CHAPTER 24

From Birth to Death

The summer months passed quickly, as fast as possible for anyone awaiting a new baby. In the meantime, following several baby showers, I had worked my last day at the bank. Gary and I settled down as prospective parents, with me waiting for the first sign of labor pains. I, for now, put aside the horrible thoughts I had experienced that Sunday afternoon at my parent's house when Papa was ill. He, for the time being, seemed to be holding his own and Mama's excitement concerning her first great-grandchild seemed to overshadow any concern she had for him at the time. I wouldn't allow myself to even think of him that afternoon or the thoughts that one day I might be asked to leave my child with them. I shuddered at the possibility of that and made a vow to God and to my unborn child that it would never happen.

On September 7th, shortly before midnight, I had my first labor pains. We made a hurried call, informing the immediate family we were on our way to the hospital. My excitement peaked as did my pain. All I could think of was that nothing could hurt that much and yet bring about anything positive. I had heard stories of how painful it was, by then I believed them. Once I had arrived in my hospital room I could only focus on watching the clock that seemed to creep from one minute to the next. At about five o'clock in the morning, the doctor finally came in and decided that he would give me something to alleviate my discomfort. The next thing I knew Gary was standing beside me saying, "Honey, we have a daughter." I groggily took his hand and managed to stifle back a tear. I was so tired and just needed to rest.

It seemed like an eternity until I got a glimpse of a nurse with a small bundle in her arms. Warm thoughts flooded me as I recalled my mother's story of a nurse bringing me to her, a little more than twenty two years earlier. "Wow, I thought!" She looks just like Gary. The nurse placed the tiny baby gently in my arms and left me to get acquainted with her. I did the usual motherly things, like carefully count each finger and toe to be sure they were all there. To my relief they were and our child was perfect.

I loved the name we had picked out, or rather the one Gary had selected. He had a niece named Dawn Marie so it was decided our first daughter would be called Shawn Marie, after her cousin. Sandy his sister was elated when Gary told her of this plan. We held our breath to see if Mama would approve. She did surprisingly, but Mother and I were both prepared to let Gary handle that issue had she not. We realized that he wasn't going to change his mind anyway and could be just as stubborn as Mama when he chose to be.

There had never been a conflict on what we would call our daughter, although Mama pointed out that she hated nicknames or abbreviations and that we should call her Shawn Marie and not just Shawn. I was thankful she didn't call me by both of my birth names. Sarah Claudette seemed a bit long plus the fact that some at school had shortened my name to Claudie and there had even been a teacher there who had mistakenly called me Caludette. I had corrected her on more than one occasion but became convinced she wasn't going to change and so had decided to just ignore that fact. I really did not like my name but then I had not been the one who had chosen it.

It had been pointed out to me many times that I was the name-sake of Claude Clayton Weathers, my mother's real father. He had died several years before I was born. Mother reminded me of this again as she stood by my bed at the hospital admiring her first grand-daughter. "I so wish my father had lived to see you and Shawn," she wistfully reminisced. "You would have loved him Claudette." She again repeated all the stories I had heard many times before about what a hard worker he had been, a pharmacist in Greenville, South Carolina, and although he did have a drinking problem had never missed a day's work. Then she would always emphasize the fact that he drank because of Mama's constant nagging.

Her stories always ended up the same way with the horrifying tale of Grandpa Claude holding her underneath the water in a river near their home. I never knew what to say when mother got to that part. I could always sense the desperation in her voice when she related that particular memory as well as the question that I sensed she was still asking, "Why would my father try to drown me?" This experience had left an indelible impression on her mind and a morbid fear of water.

Even with the knowledge of such a despicable act, she held such a reverence for him and there was always softness in her voice when she mentioned his name. I didn't know how to feel about that aspect of her life, and when it came to what children were supposed to feel about abuse, I would command my mind to shut down and therefore suppress any further thoughts on the matter. After all, things like this had happened most of my life and I always assumed that it was just the way which adults treated children.

I knew that it was inevitable that Mama and Papa would visit me in the hospital, and on Tuesday morning they both arrived. By then I was strong enough to walk to the nursery with them. Even though I was physically able to walk from my room, I was not in any way emotionally prepared for the cutting words my grandfather proclaimed as he looked at the tiny baby through the window. "Papa's going to love you just like he did your mommy," he spoke softly as he placed both hands against the glass. He glanced back at me with almost a sneer. Had he been observant he would have seen all the blood drain from my face. I felt faint. It was then that I made a hasty retreat to my room and with each step a fresh resolve came that I would never allow Shawn to stay in their home, not even for a moment.

A few days later, Gary drove me back to our mobile home where we painstakingly placed our tiny infant in her crib. The first few months of being a mother were probably the hardest, especially in the area of losing sleep. There were the two o'clock feedings that sometimes lasted for what seemed like hours. By the time I got Gary off to work in the mornings, I found it very inviting to sneak a few minutes sleep. I had devised a plan which would keep Shawn napping a little longer. At one of my baby showers someone had given me a very thin, soft blanket, and I now discovered that, if tucked right underneath her shoulders, it would keep her from flinging her hands around and pulling out her pacifier. Although this was creative, it brought a few frowns from family members who felt that she looked like a little embalmed mummy and were concerned about the way in which it restricted her as well. She looked happy enough to me, glancing around the room, without a care in the world. I refused to accept any guilt for that one. The deep circles under my eyes told the story that young mothers know only too well. I was tired and had to get some rest come what may.

With each new day life should have been getting back to normal following Shawn's birth but the fact was it remained very compli-cated. I began to struggle even more with my anger issues. My mom again suggested that I see yet another psychiatrist. The truth was, I really needed someone to say I wasn't just going through another phase that I would eventually grow out of. I hadn't grown out of any of my phases since I was a young girl and the temptation to self abuse was ever present. I didn't share with Mother to what degree I was struggling but she had, through the years, known me so well that it wasn't even necessary. She only knew that something was wrong. She again contacted Dr. White, the same psychiatrist that had seen me while I was at college and he agreed to begin sessions again. I knew that no matter what the outcome was, that I would never agree to go back to the state hospital again. I could even visualize men in 'white coats' carrying me away screaming and kicking while Gary, with tear filled eyes, stood at the door holding Shawn.

I tried to find comfort in God's Word but nothing seemed to work. I was depressed and worn out and I went through the motions of trying to be a good mother and wife but deep inside I was hurting. It was on a Friday that I had an appointment to see Dr. White. Mother suggested that Mama look after Shawn but I absolutely refused. "Claudette, she's getting older and it would mean a lot if you would let her babysit," Mother pleaded. "No!" I sharply replied, not taking my eyes off Shawn who was sleeping comfortably in her cedar rocker, the special one Mama had bought shortly before her birth. Mother gave me a sullen look but quickly gave up because she knew that there was no way I was going to change my mind. She had learned to choose her battles carefully, especially when she observed me in one of my determined moods. These had been frequent over the past few months. I had thought at one point during the conversation that she might possibly ask why I was so adamant, but she never did.

I breathed a sigh of relief because that was an issue I did not want to discuss and if I had, I wasn't at all sure I would know what to say. The mere suggestion from Gary of even visiting there on weekends sent me into a tailspin and I would find my mind traveling along that familiar path to those places of safety I had created as a young child. I was twenty-two years old by then and I had much practice in finding and securing those places. I contemplated for a moment how God could fit into all of this. There were so many answers I just didn't have and anticipated that Dr. White wouldn't either, although to appease Mother I would give therapy a try.

The next turn of events happened so fast. We got news on Monday that Mama had to send Papa to a hospital in Augusta. He had awakened and had tried to get out of bed but was unable to. She called Dr. Poliakoff, who in turn made arrangements for him to be transported to the Veteran's Hospital in Georgia. I had heard my grandmother relate stories that Papa had been in the same war as Grandpa Claude. They were even in the same infantry and also bore the same initials. Her first husband, Claude Clayton Weathers and second husband, Christopher Columbus Wilkinson had a lot in common, not least the fact that they had both fallen in love with my grandmother. One I never did meet, the other I had wished many times I had not met and now he was lying ill in a hospital bed. I felt numb because of all that had transpired in the past. Gary suggested that we should visit him immediately. I didn't respond at all to that suggestion but instead continued folding the clothes which had just been laundered. We never did make the visit and early Easter Sunday Morning on April 6, 1969 the phone rang. My grandmother called to tell us Papa was dead.

Shawn was almost seven months old when we received word of the death of Christopher Columbus Wilkinson, the one everyone in Abbeville had referred to as Johnny for years. I had often wondered why he had been given such a famous name but yet chose to be called Johnny. The name Chris would have made more sense. The obituary had said local barber for over thirty years. I pondered on what a person's obituary would be like if one were truly labeled for who they really were. I shook my head in disbelief for all the years I had feared this man, and could only be thankful that the precious little baby sleeping in the next room would never have to go through what I had. I was exceptionally quiet when the family met that evening at Mama's house to discuss funeral arrangements. Mama was not taking his death at all well and seemed to be clinging to me more than ever. She had always seemed to be melodramatic, often passing out at the first hint of distress; a trait that I was later accused of developing. She did manage to maintain a degree of composure, however, apart from one occasion when she slipped off to the bathroom to sit on the edge of the tub for half an hour staring blankly into space.

Being at this house was difficult and when Mama gave her camera to Aunt Ruth, asking her to take pictures of Johnny in his casket the following day, I felt as if I was going to be physically ill. I encouraged Gary to leave as soon as possible because I wanted to get out of that house as quickly as I could. There were plenty of family members left there to console Mama and having a seven month old was excuse enough to leave early, especially in lieu of the fact that the next day was going to be a very busy one. We had made plans to let a couple, from my mom and dad's church, look after Shawn during the time of the funeral and the long drive to the cemetery in Greenville, where Papa would be buried.

At both times when the family met, prior to the services at the funeral home, I refused to go inside. My grandmother was not at all happy with me but I firmly stood my ground. There was no way that I could bring myself to look at my grandfather in his casket. My mind argued with itself concerning this and considered the logic that to see him would be concrete proof that he was really dead; that it wasn't just some kind of devious scam to lull me into a false sense of security. But still I could not force myself to do it, no matter how reasonable or profitable that act seemed to be. I just could not get my body to obey what my mind was advising me. I stood rooted to the spot outside the home while the family received friends inside. At times like this the men usually congregated outside on the front porch so it could have appeared I had likewise just stepped out for a breath of fresh air. I didn't care in the least what others thought. I was secretly rejoicing inside that Papa was dead. I had waited for this day for many years. I had prayed for it on more than one occasion and I could now bask in the realization that he could never hurt me or any of my family again.

On the day of the funeral, as the family met inside to say their last goodbyes to Papa, Johnny, Christopher Columbus, or however they referred to him in their life, I was there alone with my thoughts. I reflected on whatever memories I could then bring to mind, and the ones that I couldn't, were again pushed back to a lower level of consciousness. These were known only to the multiple 'pockets' that my mind had, through various survival techniques, managed to create.

There were times when I could not remember what I had done the day before and the girls would often chime in unison, using their favorite expression, "Earth calling mommy!" …

CHAPTER 25

A Mother's Dilemma

The days and months following my grandfather's death were spent in a fog-like state. My feelings and emotions were jumbled and the guilt that I continued to pour on myself from that Sunday afternoon was immense. My heart went out to my grandmother, who seemed to be in a grief stricken world of her own. The only way she was able to make any sense out of what had happened over the last forty years of her life was to paint Papa as being a hero in her eyes and the eyes of all who knew him. She reminded me constantly of how much he had loved me. Even though I felt for her loss, I avoided being around her because of the haunting fear of coming to grips with the suppressed memories.

In the midst of all that was going on Gary announced that he would be starting college to get his degree in 'Drafting and Design Technology'. Since he had served in the Navy he was eligible to get assistance through the Veteran's Administration so he concluded that it would be foolish for him not to take advantage of such a wonderful opportunity. I was excited at the prospect although a little apprehensive about filling the time on my own as Gary would be studying most evenings. He was going to be covering the basic courses at Piedmont Technical College but would need to transfer to Lander University to study further. He knew that by attending college in the evenings it would take approximately five years to get his degree. Within a year I had become very frustrated at the routine we had developed. Warmed-up dinners and evenings alone became a common occurrence. I knew Gary was doing this for the benefit of our family but still it was difficult and I longed for his companionship.

I was still seeing Dr. White but was getting nowhere. I felt uneasy that my mom was investing so much money in my therapy, but on the other hand was aware of her resolve to see me set free from the horrific depression that I suffered from almost constantly. Mother would send Bonnie, my sister, over to spend the night with me as often as she was able to drag her away from her friends in Abbeville. This was a necessary diversion and it helped me get my mind off of the things that were going on in my life. To most that knew me or saw me at church, I gave the impression that everything was normal but it wasn't. The voices became louder, the nightmares became stronger and I was taking several different medications for depression. In spite of this I always made sure that Shawn was taken care of adequately. Even though my anxiety was great my maternal instinct appeared to be greater.

When Shawn was eighteen months old I discovered I was pregnant again. We were excited that she would have a brother or sister to grow up with. The fact that I had been an only child for ten years played a big part in our decision to have another child at that time. Even though I had some reservations, especially with the type of medications I had been prescribed, my doctor informed me of those drugs which should be avoided from then on.

Four months into my second pregnancy, Gary and I both decided that we needed a larger place to live in and so we purchased a new mobile home that met our requirements for extra space. I was a little disappointed since I really had my heart set on building a new house. Gary said that we were not yet financially able to do so but within a few years we could be. I had learned quickly that Gary possessed the ability to manage our finances well and even though there were times I wanted to rebel against his authority, he always had the money to pay the bills as they came due. Left on my own, I tended to be an impulse buyer whereas Gary thought things through more carefully.

Our new lot at the mobile home park was adjacent to our old one and so transferring our possessions from one to the other was relatively easy. I was able to get Mother to take care of Shawn so she would not be under our feet on our moving day. Following the relocation of the majority of our belongings and after personally carrying, what seemed like, endless bags of clothing and heavy boxes I began to have painful cramps. Gary immediately called my doctor who, after examining me, strongly suggested that I needed to rest for a few days because my body was threatening a miscarriage. I was devastated at the thought of that. I had safely carried this baby through the first trimester and I certainly didn't want anything to happen then. I lay in the bed as advised by the doctor and used the time to pray that God would protect our unborn child. After a few days I began to feel stronger but, through that experience, had learned my lesson and let Gary and my dad do the heavier work. We were not taking any further chances. The rest of the pregnancy proceeded without any further complications.

On January 8th, about mid-morning, I began to feel an unusual pressure in my body. There was not a lot of pain involved but, as it was so close to my due date, I thought it best to pay the doctor a visit so that he could at least check me over. I called Mother who wasted no time getting to Greenwood. She put Shawn's car seat into Daddy's car so he could take her back to Abbeville and in less than an hour we were both sitting in Dr. Bishop's office. At the time he was busy delivering another baby elsewhere at the hospital. While we were waiting I was assured repeatedly that the doctor would return soon. With each passing moment I became more impatient and felt this intense pressure increasing in the lower part of my back. Finally I walked up to the desk and emphatically blurted to the secretary, "I hope that you know how to deliver a baby because I think this one is on its' way!" I spoke with great urgency.

Immediately they sent Mother and me over to the hospital. The nurse who had been assigned tried hard to convince me that they needed to follow the normal procedures prior to the birth. While trying not to be rude I still spoke a little sharply, "I don't want to be the one to tell you this but we just don't have time for all that." I had already made a quick call to Gary who pleadingly asked me to wait until he got there. I chuckled inside as I thought of the tremendous effort that would be required to comply with his wishes. Within thirteen minutes of our arrival at the hospital I was being wheeled into the delivery room. Gary barely had time to sit down in the waiting area before the doctor came in and informed him he had a daughter.

This experience, although many years ago, still remains vivid in my mind. I remember screaming desperately for the nurses and they came running into the room to help me get on a gurney. It seemed only seconds before a mask was placed over my face and as I succumbed to the influence of the gas, I felt myself drop into a deep, dark hole. I wasn't sure if I had hollered out the words, "Oh No!" or not but whether audible or inaudible they expressed my fear of being in hell, the place of the damned. As I look back on this experience I am more than convinced that it was brought on by the effects of the gas. As much as I struggled to erase that picture from my mind I was not able to do so. Several times while in the hospital I had severe panic attacks, and every time I fell asleep, I again felt like I was sinking down into that hole, desperate, hopeless, and doomed to an eternal torment. In my mind associations were being made to another hole, just as deep, just as frightening as the one I had envisioned when I was being put to sleep. The events all those years earlier in the woods had left a lasting impression in my memory.

I seriously began to doubt my salvation and the God whose love was supposed to be there to sustain me. The scripture I had read many times indicated there was no place that I could go to escape His love, but on that eighth day of January I had totally felt abandoned by the God of the universe in much the same way that I felt abandoned on those lonely nights at my grandparent's house. Following this experience, even while still in the hospital, when the nurses brought Shannon into the room for her to be fed I refused to even hold her. She was such a beautiful baby, as beautiful as our first daughter, but each time I tried to reach out to her, there would be this paralyzing and gripping fear that prevented me from doing so. I felt like a total failure as a mother and wondered how I would cope once at home, especially while Gary was still attending college.

One time during my hospital stay a psychiatrist was called in because of my emotional instability. At one point I was told that I was irrational while speaking in a child's voice. Later, when home, my mom contacted Dr. White again and made arrangements for me to see him. For several months after Shannon was born Mother would come to stay us and help take care of the children. Apparently, much of the time, I would just sit on the couch staring into space and then to complicate matters further developed a severe kidney infection that lingered.

This was a particularly difficult time for Gary, Mother, Shawn, and especially the tiny baby who was being given no opportunity to bond with the one who had given birth to her. Several months later, and after I was prescribed very strong anti-depressants, Mother made plans to leave so that I could get acquainted with our new daughter. I was terrified of this prospect and for days afterwards Shannon cried way into the night. She had definitely bonded with her grandmother during their long periods of being together whereas my touch and presence was apparently foreign to her. Gary was doing all that he could, sterilizing bottles and fulfilling other necessary responsibilities whenever he wasn't studying. In addition he helped to think of creative ways to keep our two year old occupied.

There was a couple, in the church we attended, who seemed to take a special interest in us as a family. For me, it was so refreshing to be able to talk to the wife about some of the things that were going on in my life at that time. Alice soon became an important mentor in my life. Her husband David was a doctor in the town and they both lived exemplary lives, passing those same principles on to their children also. She would invite me over to their home and we would often spend time designing and sewing new clothes for ourselves. In addition to this, Mother was always more than happy to have Shawn and Shannon staying at her house on special occasions, as she had missed them so much after returning home, following her extended stay with us. Both the actions of Alice and Mother helped to alleviate some of the pressure on me.

Through my special friends, Alice and David, I began to understand the unconditional love of Jesus. Alice knew the struggles I was going through and, although not able to completely understand the concept of disassociation, she always showed me through God's Word those simple truths of His love and sufficiency for my life. She also encouraged me to memorize scripture in order to strengthen my Christian walk. As I look back now, I am reminded of the ways in which God brings people into our lives who then touch us in such significant ways. God had once again visited me in a similar manner to those times in the pasture behind Mrs. Fuller's house. This time, however, His presence was through people He had strategically placed in my path. It was many years later when I fully got the picture of all that Christ had done for me.

For the next few years my emotions partially leveled out although at times there seemed to be a constant shadow following me, dragging me down into a bottomless pit from where there seemed to be no escape. I had learned during those times of despair and fear how to deceive others into thinking I was experiencing a perfect tranquil life. I had been taught how to do that by the master of deceit, my step grandfather. Even though he had been dead for some time, he continued to control and influence my life by the presence of an intense bitterness that I still felt for him.

Gary, in the meantime, had graduated from Lander University with honors. I brimmed over with pride as I dressed Shawn and Shannon, that Sunday afternoon, in their nicest attire to attend their father's graduation. In my estimation it had been a very long five years that he had been studying and so was excited at the prospect that I would soon have him back as a fulltime husband and father. I was determined to make my life work then and set out on a mission to be the best mother, wife, and church member in the history of mankind. It worked for quite awhile and, even though I had inward struggles, no one knew about them not even Gary. We were both attending church regularly and praying together at night before going to bed. In spite of this façade I continued to experience a gnawing dread of impending danger. Even though there were times I longed to talk to my husband about these fears; I just could not bring myself to do it.

There were times when I could not remember what I had done the day before and the girls would often chime in unison, using their favorite expression, "Earth calling mommy!" I am sure, if older, they might have also observed my rather odd blank stare as I attempted to carry on a conversation with them. If challenged, I would have just attributed it to having a lot on my mind. Gary seemed oblivious to what was going on during those times. His focus was working a forty hour week and I had more than once detected that he was under a lot of pressure at work. I felt that listening to my problems was the last thing that he needed to do. Instead I followed my usual practice of covering up my secrets in any way that I could. This only sufficed for so long; soon my past began to catch up with me and was suppressed no longer.

The girls were getting old enough to realize something was very wrong but it was as if there was a large obstacle sitting in the living room which, even though every member of the household tripped over it, no one had the courage to admit it existed ...

CHAPTER 26

Return to House Of Horror

Neither Gary nor I was prepared for the news that I had been given at the doctor's office that November day in 1975 but, in spite of this, we were both delighted that our third child was on the way. We had waited almost five years and this was an excellent time to complete our family. By then we both realized that buying a house was not something we could continue to put off as we had already outgrown our current space. Gary immediately began the search so that by the time I was seven months pregnant we had moved into our new home in a nice subdivision not too far from where we had lived for the past six years. With only a few months to spare Sherrie Renee' appeared on the scene weighing a little less than six pounds. Upon arriving home, my dear friend Alice was already at the house, waiting to place her in a crib in the newly furnished nursery. Our family was now complete. We had three beautiful daughters; Shawn, Shannon, and Sherrie.

By the time that Sherrie was two years old, Mother's pastor at Westside had a vision of opening a Christian School there. After it was voted on and passed by the church membership, plans were made to begin full operation the next fall. Mother was very excited because she had been asked to teach Kindergarten. She always had a way with children and being a college graduate was qualified for that type of career. She talked with me about taking Shawn out of public school and letting her, as well as Shannon, attend Westside the next year. When I discussed this with Gary he opposed it because private schools were very expensive and he was concerned that we might get into financial difficulties following our purchase of a new home. He only agreed to this arrangement after much pleading on my part and a promise that I would take on at least seven piano students in order to pay for the tuition.

I put an advertisement in the local newspaper and to my surprise seven parents answered. This seemed like 'divine affirmation' that it was God's will for the girls to attend Westside, as it was the exact number needed to cover the fees. I later discovered that the most interesting aspect in our decision to transfer the girls was the fact that someone was needed to head up the Music Department and I filled that position. Next fall the girls began at the new school and much to our delight we were able to get free tuition because I was on the faculty there. By then I was well into my new career of teaching, all day at Westside and every evening at home. I loved earning money which I could call my own; money that was not scrutinized by Gary. I was unhappy with the fact that even though we had a joint checking account he always kept the check book. We didn't see eye to eye on financial issues and so each time that money was needed for something it appeared that I was begging.

I did not view my attitude as being independent, nor did I in any way feel that I was not being submissive to my husband. The truth was Gary did not approve of me working. The number of students I had doubled from seven the first year to fourteen the following year. Each subsequent year saw another ten or so added so that by the fourth year I found myself teaching right through until eight o'clock most evenings.

Our home life suffered and the communication that Gary and I had enjoyed in the past came to an abrupt end. Before my teaching career began I had led a community bible study for a small number of women. With the teaching load I then embraced at school and at home I seemed to neglect all the concepts which God had led me to teach others in previous years. The ways in which I had honored my husband as head of the house were soon lost as my stubborn, independent will took over. How easily the enemy can deceive us and how much he desires to thwart God's divine plan for our lives. What I had initially envisioned for the girls was to have a Christian foundation and it had seemed a worthy cause at the time. The area of my life that needed improvement was clearly my independent spirit which had totally led me out of God's will. Before long I discovered the truth of the Bible where it states that even though money itself isn't evil, the love of it is and can lead a person down a wrong path.

Nothing goes right when one is out of God's will and, from the onset of my decision to put the girls in a private school, my life careened out of balance. Gary and I were worlds apart. He complained constantly that we had no home life and that was true. For a while we had been moving in different directions. He had become involved in the CB radio craze and it meant that we were both so consumed by the things we were doing that our paths rarely crossed. I taught until eight and then he spent the rest of the evening on the radio talking with friends. I was bitter because he had little time for me or the girls and he was displeased at my refusal to give up work.

I again fell into a deep depression but this time instead of depending on pills I found that alcohol numbed the pain of the loneliness that I sometimes felt. We both drank on occasion and it took me a long time to admit that it had become a crutch and that I depended on it far more often than I should. Another way of escape for me was walking. I had become obsessed with going out early in the morning for a six mile walk and then walking another six miles in the evening, riding my bicycle for another seven miles and neglecting to eat. My life was spiraling out of control and I felt that Gary's was as well. Neither of us admitted this to each other. I later ended up in the hospital for a week because I had lost too much weight. I was diagnosed with anorexia and told by my doctor that if I didn't stop purging I would most certainly die.

The girls were getting old enough to realize something was very wrong but it was as if there was a large obstacle sitting in the living room which, even though every member of the household tripped over it, no one had the courage to admit it existed. Frustrations built up and Gary changed in his behavior towards me, significantly affecting our relationship. In the same ways in which I had been betrayed as a child I was also betrayed by my husband. The choices he made and the other things he was doing at that time made me feel unsafe physically, sexually and emotionally and also made me fearful for our daughters as well. We had became a dysfunctional family; just as dysfunctional as the one in my past.

When Sherrie was nine, and Shannon and Shawn then teenagers, I could take it no more and walked out of my nineteen year marriage. I worked four jobs in order to support the girls and myself and the only thing I expected from Gary was a clean break and no reprisals. I set out to begin a new life and within a year was married again. This time I married Ray who had no clue as to what he was taking on or he may have had second thoughts. His marriage to me came with a ready-made family. He had one daughter from a previous marriage who lived with her mom and I am sure that he felt quite outnumbered with the four of us.

By this time my grandmother, being elderly and in poor health, had gone to live with my mom and dad. Mother suggested that we move into Mama's empty house so that Ray could look after the grounds. Someone had burglarized the house shortly after she had moved out and, with this being a potential problem for the future, Mother saw our moving in there as the perfect solution. Ray spent hours trying to convince me this was actually a good idea. For the first time I poured out my feelings to him; those ones I hadn't been able to share with anyone else concerning the house and how I felt about it. "Ray, I can't move in there!" "I am so afraid!" I pleaded over and over to him. He did everything in his power to reassure me, promising that he would be there and that my fears were totally unfounded. When asked why I was so apprehensive I could only tell him of always having problems in the house, day and night.

I knew Ray worked on the railroad and would be out many nights, but with each excuse I produced for not moving he seemed to come up with a more valid reason for doing so. He finally convinced me it was best and so the five of us moved in. The house, although lovely, only had two bedrooms and one bath; not very conducive to comfortable living for two adults, two teenagers and a very active nine year old.

We managed to place three single beds in one of the large bedrooms for the girls. Even though not at all pleased about this arrangement they reluctantly claimed a bed each and placed their luggage at the end of it. At first sight this gave the appearance of walking into the home of 'The Three Bears' from the familiar bedtime story. The only thing that was missing was the obvious smell of porridge in the kitchen nearby.

The girls soon adapted to their new environment as many young people do. We told them that until we were able to store Mama's clothes elsewhere; everything had to remain in its' proper place in the drawers, in the dressers and the closets. It was a bit more difficult in our bedroom as we had the smaller one of the two which only had an extremely small closet. As Ray and I had so many clothes between us, we ended up having to use racks in the living room and these were still there a year later. I was very nervous that first night back in Mama's house and found a need to distract myself from dwelling on the thoughts that our room and bed was the same one I had used as a child, knowing that if I didn't it would stir up unpleasant memories. To achieve this distraction I decided to go through some of my grandmother's belongings to determine those articles that could be thrown out.

Even though my grandmother had been an immaculate house-keeper, I knew there were some things that she certainly would want to dispose of and felt these could be placed in a box to check with Mother at a later time. I could not have imagined what I was about to find that night. Sitting on the bed I rummaged through a variety of my grandmother's belongings in the chest of drawers. Ray was busy working in the den, connecting the television, and the girls were giggling in their bedroom. There were several items scattered about, including a partially sealed white envelope which particularly grabbed my attention. I opened it and to my shock found myself staring into the face of my dead grandfather lying in his casket. I had unwittingly stumbled upon the pictures Aunt Ruth had taken. Upon seeing them I began to scream uncontrollably. I threw the pictures on the floor and ran from the bedroom. Ray was able to grab me by the arm as I passed him and spun me around. The girls stood staring at the scene as he tried to calm me down. The nightmare had begun.

"My name is Faye, and I'm a multiple."

CHAPTER 27

Fragmented Identity

The fear of that night set precedence over most of the subsequent ones spent in the country. On that occasion Ray had found the envelope and the pictures scattered about on the floor as he and the girls raced into our bedroom to find out what the commotion was all about. I made it very plain in the midst of my tears that it wasn't enough to just throw those pictures away but that he needed to immediately remove them from the house. To appease me he made a deliberate effort to walk outside and throw them onto the existing pile of trash designated to be taken to the dump the following day. The next afternoon the two of us made a special trip down the road, approximately a quarter of a mile from where we lived, to go through the ritual of specifically burning them. I stood there solemnly watching the final images of my dead grandfather curl up in the heat and be consumed in the flames. As we drove away, I looked back at the smoldering pile of ashes and wondered then if life could ever be normal again.

A few days later after me finding Papa's pictures Sherrie ask me a very odd question. "Mom, when did you start coloring?" I was clearing up breakfast dishes at the time as she proceeded to tell me of an incident that had happened the previous day. She related that on returning home from school she noticed me sitting in the middle of the living room floor coloring and speaking in a child's voice. This had been the first time that I had been confronted by one of our children about this type of behavior. I really did not know how to respond, except to ask her a question in return. "Well Sherrie, what did you do?" I asked this apprehensively as I sat down at the little kitchen table and motioned for her to join me. Instead of sitting down with me she nervously shifted from foot to foot in the middle of the room and then, without making any further comment, bolted to the den to watch television.

I sat there for quite some time reflecting on what she had said and wondering how my unpredictable actions were affecting the girls. There had been many instances where I was aware of blank spots or what I referred to as 'lost time'. Whereas these occurrences were a part of normal life for me, to others looking on they would have appeared strange. I had no recollection of sitting on the floor coloring, or talking to Sherrie while in that state of mind.

Within a week of that experience I received an unexpected telephone call from Dr. Bob Crowe, a clinical psychologist; I had first met a few years previously. At that time, he had strongly advised me to see a psychiatrist as he felt I needed far more help than he was qualified to give. I had determined from that day on I would not allow any more counselors or therapists into my situation. Most of my life had been spent going to such people with no positive results and so to further pursue this course of action seemed futile to me.

The phone call in itself proved to be a catalyst and a beginning to some of the answers I needed in my life. Dr. Crowe was quick to apologize to me for not making an accurate diagnosis at the start and asked if I would be willing to attend a seminar he was conducting at the hospital. Although no details were given I agreed to go, mostly out of curiosity. A few weeks later I sat with a group of others in the conference room at the local hospital and listened to a young woman give an account of her life. I sat spellbound for at least two hours and felt that I was looking into a mirror reflecting aspects of my own life. She spoke of the intense abuse she had suffered and how she endeavored for years to cover it up and hide it. In doing so she had lost part of her own identity and had created multiple personalities so that she could cope.

There were times when she was speaking to us that she would obviously adopt the character of another person, speaking in a different voice which was often childlike, and glancing around the room in fear. Dr. Crowe sat beside her in a consoling manner and reassured her she was safe. For the first time that afternoon, I began to make some sense of my life. The question that I kept asking myself was, what was I then to do with the new knowledge I had gained?

At the end of the seminar I thanked Dr. Crowe for his invitation and he asked if I would be interested in coming to the support group that had been set up at the hospital. I was not particularly excited about any such groups because of my association with them in the past but this time, being desperate for help, agreed to go. My first meeting was just spent listening to others share. By the time I met there for the second time, a voice within me gathered the courage to finally admit, "My name is Faye, and I'm a multiple." Claudette, my basic personality, was still around but obviously buried beneath the rubble of memories that she had so cleverly learned to suppress.

There was something absolutely liberating about this type of revelation but there was also the possibility of perhaps opening up a Pandora's Box. Looking back now I can view this experience as quite a spiritual one. My life was like a giant puzzle and the pieces, which providence had managed to scatter, could only come together again by admitting that the puzzle existed in the first place. Up until the time of that seminar, I had perceived myself to be crazy and so this was the label I had secretly claimed and felt others probably identified for me as well. The new insights gained through attending the support group meant that for the first time I could finally embrace a hope that perhaps the pieces of my fragmented life could be reassembled.

I continued attending the group each week but found that some other members were super-sensitive and therefore unable to interact in the way the support leader had hoped for. After several months, of seemingly not making any progress in that group, I felt my time there was pointless and refused to go back. Even though the DID Support Group had not worked for me, individual therapy with Dr. Crowe appeared to be more productive. He gave me something to build on and instilled the hope that my multiple personalities could somehow be integrated into one.

Integration was a term the young lady had spoken of at the seminar and, even though a vague concept to me at the time, it now became viable although scary. The most frightening thought to me was, that even though combining my personalities into one part could change my life for the better, it still might rob me of something I had always depended upon for security. In my view this could be traumatic like losing my doll confidantes had been; the ones that used to sit on the shelves of the hall closet at home so many years before. I knew that changes needed to happen in my life but just couldn't anticipate what form they would take.

The changes those next few years were major ones because both Shawn and Shannon had moved out to begin lives of their own. There was not one night that I felt comfortable following the decision to move into Mama's house. Even with Sherrie in the next room I would often wake up in distress, thinking again I was that same little girl fearing the terrors of the night. The nightmares also increased as well as the disassociation. On some occasions there were times I would actually find myself in the woods, running frantically as if pursued by someone in the darkness. Fortunately I never ventured so far from the house that I got lost, as this would have been easy to do in the vast expanse of the seventy acres we lived on. More than once I came to myself barefooted and very frightened as I looked up at the towering trees above me with the moon as my only source of light. Even though physically I was no longer under threat from my childhood tormentor there was no way to convince my mind of this and so I continued to be in a constant state of abreaction.

Ray became very aware of this problem and, being a man of great ingenuity, devised a plan to keep me inside the house at night. He assembled what appeared to be a long wind chime that hung from the top of the door which, if tampered with, would make a loud clanging sound. Sherrie found this contraption quite amusing and was warned to suppress any temptation to touch it on her way to the bathroom during the night. In spite of Ray's brilliant idea of the wind chime alarm, it appeared that one of my many personalities must have learned how to gently squeeze a few of the metal pipes together so that she could slip away undetected. As a result of this the problem continued.

If I had to expound on one experience which had the greatest impact on ending our marriage, it was the one when we both awoke to find tree branches spread out over much of the bedroom. (Trees had always been the safety-net for one of my personalities known as Kara) Ray at first just stood there surveying the situation. Then, after what seemed to be an eternity, he turned to me with a look of total shock. "Claudette, I don't understand anything about Multiple Personalities and I really don't want to." "I don't trust you anymore and have no desire to sleep with one eye open the rest of my life wondering if you might be a danger to yourself, to Sherrie, or even me. Within a few months of that incident, Ray had decided to move out into a small building at the back of the house which he converted into an apartment.

In my heart I knew from that time on that basically our marriage was over and, even though we maintained a civil relationship, Ray made it clear that he was not moving back into the house after the tree branch incident. I found it increasingly difficult to live in the country without the protective presence of my husband and so within a year I had completely stopped spending nights there and Sherrie had no alternative but to go and live with her dad. It finally came down to my inability emotionally or physically to cope as a suitable mother for my youngest daughter or as a stable wife for my husband. I decided to move in with friends in Greenwood, neither of whom was equipped to deal with the emotional problems that I had. Now in retrospect, I can see how during those periods of crisis, that my codependent nature always directed me to rely on people rather than God.

At this particular time I was not just losing hours and minutes, but weeks and months as well. There were other personalities within me who came out to handle major crisis, like my grandmother's death. There was even one who went ahead and purchased Mama's house, the very one that I myself had hated for so long. For me to try and explain to someone else, the actions of those different identities that my mind had created would have been futile. I stopped seeing Dr. Crowe and I vowed to never visit another counselor. Other than the friends I was staying with in Greenwood, few knew of how complex my life had become as a person living with multiple personalities. These were the ones who would sometimes take me to other states, driving aimlessly on dark and lonely roads at night, tormented by thoughts of suicide.

The voices in my head were sometimes louder than any thoughts could ever be and I continued to walk that same self-destructive pathway I had walked many times before. My drug and alcohol abuse became more intense although my ways of hiding it were more subtle. This practice continued for quite some time until the decision was made to enter rehab.

Even though I was desperately hurting inside, I knew there was within me a mother's heart that so wanted her daughter Sherrie back home again. Gaining her trust wouldn't be easy but I knew that if I really tried it would be possible to get free of the drug and alcohol addictions. Ridding myself of the multiple personalities, however, was a different matter altogether and was never going to be straightforward.

Within a year after Ray and I were divorced, Sherrie agreed to move back home, this time to a small apartment in Greenwood. I made plans to sell the house in the country but until I was able to find a suitable buyer, I rented it out. Sherrie also had a solemn promise from me that our lives would be different and that I would, from then on, always be there for her. That was a promise I vowed to keep. Apart from the amazing freedom of being away from that house and its memories, it was wonderful to have Sherrie back home. She was happy about being there but nothing could compare with the excitement I felt in finally having her with me again.

As I drove away from my house that day I definitely never expected to return home again but, fortunately, I was not the one driving the car ...

CHAPTER 28

Divine Appointment

I prayed that the country home would be sold quickly and that I could find another one suitable for us. It was a waste of money to rent a home and so to buy seemed much more sensible. The choice to keep the house and land surrounding it was an unattractive proposition in spite of the financial gains which had been made from the sale of timber. In retrospect it was not worth the price I had paid earlier in my life. I needed a fresh start and that was the best way that I knew of how to achieve it. Within six months the paperwork was finalized and we finally began plans to move to our new home in Greenwood, one with space for a music studio to fulfill a long held dream of mine. It was the perfect location and Sherrie and I were both thrilled to move in. She was going to work part time in addition to attending the local college. Sherrie had made a decision to become an electrical engineer, thus following a similar career to her father.

To this day she still mentions to me about the times that I would surprise her with a special breakfast in bed on some weekends and also my very odd habit of folding her dirty laundry on days she didn't have time to clean her room. "Mom, it is one thing to fold clean clothes but quite another to fold the dirty ones," she would jokingly say to me. In later years we laughed about that one and I was pleased to have been able to create some happy memories for her.

Sherrie and I spent a few really good years together there but, as with all young people, the time came for her to venture out on her own. On that occasion her departure was quite different than it had been before. She was the last daughter living at home since both of the older girls were married by then with families of their own. Sherrie needed her independence but there was going to be an incredible void left by her absence.

Shawn suggested that on the weekend that Sherrie planned to move into her apartment, we should take a trip to Florida, which would help with the transition process. It was a great idea and we both looked forward to a change of scenery as well. Her mother-in-law invited us to stay with her and we were all excited about going. It turned out to be a wonderful week but on returning home I remember that overwhelming feeling of loneliness and emptiness as I entered the house knowing that Sherrie was gone. She was just across town but it felt as if we were countries apart.

For some reason it had occurred to me that loving someone ultimately meant that person would walk away. I looked upon my life as one that had portrayed that particular aspect time and time again. It started with my mom who left me at my grandparent's house on weekends, my father's abrupt death at age thirty five, and two failed marriages as well as the girls one by one forging a new life centered around their friends and own families. The abuse experienced in the past represented a great loss in much the same way as the other situations in which people disappeared from my life one by one.

I found myself very angry with a God who seemed to allow children to be abused or abandoned and disappointed with my own inability to accept even normal life changes. Just as desperately as I had many times held on to the expensive dolls in my hall closet, there was an intense obsession to cling on to family members, friends, or anything else that was an emotional prop.

Could it be that for the first time I was actually recognizing within myself a consuming selfishness, the kind that often lingers with the carnal nature each of us possesses, even after salvation? I had certainly not been ready to turn my life over to a God who I hadn't yet learned how to trust.

I don't believe in a secular concept of fate but it was on August 26, 2002, that I had a divine appointment. My interpretation of fate would be a secular happening that appeared out of nowhere which had a profound influence upon your life but without any spiritual benefit. Having a divine appointment, on the other hand, would mean the exact opposite and would have eternal significance. Up until this point in my life nothing had made a lot of sense to me except that its course had followed one unhappy experience after another and I remained unconvinced that God really cared for me. I had been thinking again of obvious ways of ending my life as I had done many times before. On one particular day, I came to the conclusion that life was really not worth living and made the decision that I was going to leave no room for error this time. There would be no more botched suicide attempts. Having settled this in my mind, I took what I thought to be a final look at the house bought several years previously.

This decision wasn't about Sherrie growing up and moving out as the other girls had done, because that was just one of those 'inevitables', so didn't come as a big surprise. This time being alone wasn't the main problem. I now faced something far greater than I could ever have anticipated. I had gone through rehab and found that I could live without drugs and alcohol. I had finally managed to have self control in many areas of my life but I had also made a statement to God with regards to the seven personalities within me, and that was, "God, this is as good as it is going to get." Just like that little girl who refused to give up her dolls to a younger sister, I was again faced with the question; when would I be willing to give up my special identities? I knew that surrendering those parts of me which had provided security as a child could possibly now be destroying me as an adult. The truth was that I couldn't make Jesus Lord of my life as long as I had something else that I depended on more than Him.

My years of reckless living had finally caught up with me also. I was bankrupt in every sense of the word and it wasn't all about finances. Even though my bank account was nearly empty it was not half as empty as my soul. I was still letting everything be about me, my problems, my thoughts, my injustices and virtually none of it was.

As I drove away from my house that day I definitely never expected to return home again but, fortunately, I was not the one driving the car and neither was it any of my personalities. God had control of the steering wheel that day. Instead of driving to an isolated location and waiting for a stale bottle of tranquilizers to do their job, I found myself in the parking lot of a church. I literally ran into the office and cried out for help. I was immediately taken into the sanctuary where a lady, who worked there, talked and prayed with me until the pastor arrived. I spoke with him for about an hour and his suggestion was for me to talk to a man named Dave, who was a counselor at the church. I was thinking at the time that the last person I wanted to talk to was yet another counselor but because of my desperate state I agreed to do so.

It took me four hours that day to tell Dave my story and the strange thing was, the first statement I made to him was this, "I don't trust you." He looked at me with a kind look on his face and replied, "That's ok, and I am willing to earn that trust." I only had to tell Dave my story once. I did not have to relive the horror of it over and over as I had done so many times, through the years, when seeing other counselors and therapists. One of the things that impressed me about Dave was the fact that he would not allow me to stay focused on my past as others had done. As he began to work with me I saw something that I had never seen before, and that was hope and a way out of that miserable life, not through suicide but through the miraculous work of the great 'Bondage Breaker', Jesus Christ.

Dave never condemned me but continually assured me of the amazing love of God; a love that was so great that He had brought me to that hour and place in my life. Dave talked about God being a gentleman who neither would force anything on me that I did not want, nor enter anywhere He wasn't invited. I could see how I had in the past allowed authority figures to distort my thinking about God and to generate a fear that He would forsake me and hurt me as others had done. It was approximately two weeks later, after first meeting with Dave, that I prayed a sincere prayer releasing to God my past, the remaining personalities, and anything else that was exalting itself above Him. Something miraculous happened to me that afternoon in Dave's office. I was set free, not only of my past but also of depression, self abuse and Multiple Personality Disorder. As I lifted my hands in prayer I felt a weight fall from my shoulders. This had nothing to do with anything that Dave had done, or anything that I had done, but was entirely because of what Christ had achieved on the cross for me.

In the Bible it states,' Therefore, my beloved, as you have always obeyed, not as in my presence only, but now much more in my absence, work out your own salvation with fear and trembling." I began to see what the scripture meant in that powerful passage and in the following days and months I also began to see who I was in Christ and what my purpose in life was. I had never been able to view myself as a saint because I couldn't get past the sinner part. To my amazement I discovered, while on an internet chat program called Paltalk, that there were many more who felt very much as I did. I am certain that God led me to install this program on my computer and, along with everything that had happened prior to doing so, was part of His Divine plan for me. There were many who, like me, had given up hope of ever being a whole person again. All didn't have the label of MPD/DID, or were even self abusers as I had been, but one common factor was that they had all been needy children and many had also been deprived of the agape love of God. Those malnourished in that way were left with a void in their hearts which they themselves had been unable to fill.

As I began to interact with people online, God began to do something miraculous in my own life because the more I reached out to others the less I thought about me. The focus had been on my problems in the past and I had allowed bitterness to consume me. I knew that in order to be completely whole again it would be necessary to release those who had injured me. Because I was convinced that God had the answer for those wounded by their past, I chose 'Life After Abuse' for the name of the chat room I opened. It was and still remains my constant prayer that others will be set free as I had been.

I found out there was no miracle cure in the practices of the secular psychiatric world, because if anyone had tried that route, I had. No formula of man's, whether it be a drug, method, or institution was going to be the complete answer to man's spiritual needs as nothing compared to the work that Christ did on the cross. This was the answer and although I knew that I was not going to suddenly reach perfection, I was well on my way to a life free from the bondages of my past. Dave's encouragement to use the internet as a means of ministry proved positive in a variety of ways. It provided many with a safe and progressive means of expressing past hurts without fear or condemnation. It gave hope for the future through the completed work of Jesus, and it was a way we could share the Gospel throughout the world.

* See Philippians 2:12

EPILOGUE

I stand in awe of what God has done and how He has worked miraculously, taking those negative aspects of my life and using them for His glory. Many times I have meditated on the verses of Psalm 139, considering how God in all of His divine wisdom knew all about my life before even a day of it had begun. He had a master plan and even though the enemy tried to kill, steal, and destroy those things that God wanted for me, I have emerged victorious in Him. I not only intellectually know the 'God of the Pasture', but He is now my intimate Friend and He walks with me daily. He is my Guide, Provider, Strength and my All in All.

I am reminded again and again that nothing takes God by surprise and, even though we do go through some intense trials and tribulations, we all make choices in how we respond to each situation. We can ultimately either let the difficulties make us bitter or better. For many years I struggled with issues of anger and a refusal to forgive those who had wounded me. Because of my inability to see God's plan in the midst of what had happened, I missed out on many of the blessings that He had for me and for a long time was powerless to use my experiences to help others as well.

Maturity in the Lord doesn't come overnight. I am still in process and will continue to be as long as I live. I have doubted many things in my life but never again will I doubt God's amazing love, grace and protection of me during my childhood. Even though His grace is amazingly free it cost the Father the life of His only Son and there is a cost to us as well. That cost is the willingness to die to our own selfish desires and wholly surrender to the One who did so much for us.

I spent many years wandering in the 'wilderness of my mind', much in the same way as the children of Israel did on their journey to the Promised Land. Like them, I grumbled and complained and even after being set free I had to also trust God to handle the giants that the enemy continued to send my way. I am thankful that the curse of abuse, which resulted in mistrust, depression, self abuse and MPD/DID, was finally broken by the powerful name of Jesus Christ. I am also thankful each new day that Jesus did what no psychiatrist, method, institution or medication could ever do.

For whatever reason it existed in the first place, I do praise God for my mind's creative ability to disassociate. Without that way of escape, I doubt very seriously if I would be alive today. As a young girl I experienced firsthand many wrongs committed by people who I should have been able to trust in my life. I am thoroughly convinced that even though God never ordained that any wrongs should have happened to me, or to any of His creation, injustices happen. Because of free will people make wrong decisions and as a result innocent people are often hurt.

At eleven years old I witnessed mans' inhumanity to man and especially to the black race at the hands of the KKK. It sickens me even today to think that anyone would hate another because of the color of their skin. Growing up in the south, I witnessed an era where a society felt the need to have; one water fountain for the white race and yet another for the black, separate schools for the children, separate doctor's waiting rooms and restaurants where the blacks were not allowed to enter. My heart is still saddened to think of a young boy or girl whose father didn't return home that fateful night. Many families lost fathers or brothers this way, and few black people were rarely taken seriously if they reported a loved one missing. Only in these last few years have the blacks been free to tell their side of the story. God is changing all of that.

I thank God for the love He gave me for the black race and for the healing that I have seen the last few years, especially in Abbeville, South Carolina. I am so thankful to my pastor, Dr. Wendell Rhodes for his vision in bridging the racial gap in the town where so much brutality took place. The sweet peace of reconciliation resounds over and over as both black and white worship together each week at the Friendship Praise and Worship Center. Again we have been touched by the great Bondage Breaker Jesus Christ.

As a Christian, I have forgiven all of the abusers in my life. I truly believe that if a person wants freedom then they must forgive, not half heartedly but sincerely out of a desire to be obedient to God. Forgiveness is as clear a choice as that of accepting Jesus as ones' personal Savior. We must be quick to forgive others as He commanded. God wants to bless us and to bless others. The curse of racial barriers is being broken. The roots of bitterness perpetuated by each generation kept it active far too long. We are 'One' under God and in the body of Christ as we walk together hand in hand, not as a race but as fellow believers in Christ claiming His love, power and truth.

Each Tuesday and Friday night I meet with a special group of people who, like me, have struggled with past issues of abuse; most have been abused but come seeking a better way to deal with the hurts of their past. I know that God called me into this ministry on September 19, 2002 and this past September we celebrated six years on Paltalk. Our initials now say LAAMI which signifies Life After Abuse Ministries International. We have moderators in Canada, the UK and the United States that help us in providing a safe environment for those who need help in overcoming problems resulting from past abuses.

I am reminded again of the thirty-five hurting people who came into the internet chat room that first time a little over six years ago. I stayed up most of the night listening to, and praying with, those who came into 'Life After Abuse'. For most of them they, like me, had given up and felt there was no place to go. Most were depressed and some were self abusive as I had been most of my life. It was evident they needed a safe place where they could learn to trust again. This was a wonderful opportunity to provide such a place. Thus 'Life After Abuse' began. We continue to see the fruits of this ministry in those who have joined us. Many have not just listened to the studies we cover but have also allowed their lives to be changed by them.

Some of these have moved on in other areas of ministry. Some have joined LAAMI as moderators.

I will never forget the Saturday afternoon shortly after 'Life After Abuse' opened when a young woman from England happened to come into the room while we were doing some basic maintenance online. We ended up leading her to Jesus. I received a Christmas card from her a few years ago, thanking me for being obedient to God and relating how her life had drastically changed since she came to know Jesus. I am totally convinced that she had a divine appointment in much the same way I did that afternoon in Dave's office. I am excited about what God has done and is going to continue to do through this ministry and in the lives of others who are involved with it.

In closing, I want to leave you with the hope that whatever you may be struggling with, God wants to help you. He is there waiting for you to pour out your heart to Him. Give Him your hurt, your past, your tears, and when you take that step of faith He will do exactly what He has promised. He will set you free. Accept His freedom. Live in the victory that can be yours. All you abused neglected, and abandoned children know this, God loves you! You will then be freed to tell your own story and will also have the liberty to share with others that they too can be healed by the 'Great Bondage Breaker'.

John 8:32, 36 And ye shall know the truth, and the truth shall make you free ..... If the Son therefore shall make you free, ye shall be free indeed.

Printed in the United States
213083BV00002B/1/P

9 781607 913665